Regaining Control

Clinician's Guide

James E. Rogers

WritePsych Publishing LLC.

ISBN-13: 978-1719352475
ISBN-10: 171935247X

First printing 2018.

WritePsych Publishing LLC.

This book is dedicated to the guys
who taught me so much.

Contents

vii

Introduction and Background

Regaining Control: Winning the Battle Against Sexually Abusive Behavior (*Regaining Control*) grew out of my experience treating sex offenders. Through many hours of conducting group and individual therapy, it became clear to me that though clients had some characteristics in common—impulsivity and lack of considering consequences of actions to name two—they each had unique histories and needs.

Regaining Control, attempts to address these differences in client's experience by breaking client treatment programs into two parts. Part 1 of *Regaining Control* focuses on the thoughts and feelings that are common to most offenders (and most humans for that matter). It considers topics such as the struggle between the "emotional brain" and the "executive brain." The first section of the workbook looks at the way emotions can overpower healthy thinking. In my experience, most clients say that at the time of their offense, they weren't thinking. They say their actions were out of character, and some men look back on their actions with a sense of disbelief. Part 1 addresses the relationship between thoughts, feelings, and behaviors as clients examine their offense.

Part 2 of the workbook considers a broad range of topics that are tailored to individual client needs. Chapters explore topics such as sexual schema, pornography, rape, empathy, ethics, sexual relationships, purpose, and cycles of behavior. *Regaining Control* uses client input to establish a course of treatment. This results in clients who are more engaged, since they feel the program is more tailored to them as individuals.

Approach

One objective of *Regaining Control* is to provide treatment that is informative in a compassionate environment. It does this by using a new model to address the client's experience. The workbook talks of the role of the "emotional" and "executive" brains. It acknowledges that we all struggle with emotional impulses, and can all benefit from the exercise of executive control. It views sexual offenses as examples of the same two-brain conflict that is evidenced in many other areas of our lives.

This emotional-versus-executive brain approach fits very closely with clients' experience. Again, most said they weren't thinking at the time of their offense. In the terms of the workbook, when they committed their offense, their emotional brain was in control. It should be noted that the workbook is not intended to diminish the positive contributions of emotions. It stresses that emotions are a valid and valuable part of our experience. It simply says that emotions (especially when intense) must also be experienced under the guidance of the executive brain with its ability to plan, anticipate consequences, and rein in emotions when they might lead us into trouble.

Brains and Offenses

The workbook assumes that client conduct is the result of brain activity. While this might seem obvious, it serves as the foundation of the workbook. It further assumes that brain activity is the product of the complex interplay between the brain and the body. This is perhaps nowhere more evident than in the experience of sex. Sexual arousal leads to dramatic changes in brain function. Similarly, brain function (attending to sexual stimuli, imagining sexual experience, etc.) have related physiological responses.

Regaining Control hopes to increase client awareness of the interplay between mind and body with the hope that clients will be able to intentionally manage emotional states. Furthermore, it is hoped that by exercising control of emotional states, they may in fact be strengthening the structures of the brain that make control more possible. Sexual misconduct is viewed as a deficit of learning rather than just a moral failure.

Terminology

Executive Brain: The executive brain and its operations are extensively discussed. The executive brain is roughly equivalent physiologically with the prefrontal cortex—the brain center that plans, anticipates and evaluates consequences of behavior. It is the root of logical thought and sets goals and determines strategies to accomplish them. Throughout the workbook, the executive brain's role in regulating emotions is emphasized.

Emotional Brain: In *Regaining Control,* the emotional brain is roughly equivalent to the limbic system with its generation of emotional states. Emotions are considered to be a valuable aspect of human experience, but it is emphasized that they are unreliable when used as the basis for decision making and action. The emotional brain's influence on sexual behavior is extensively discussed.

Who the Workbook is For

This workbook is intended to be used in treatment with male offenders. This is partly due to that fact that men comprise the vast majority of sexual offenders. It is also focused on men because men have significant differences in the motivations that lead to sexually offending. This is not to say that females don't commit sexual offenses—some male clients have been their victims. It is simply to say that treatment for female offenders differs enough to warrant a treatment approach better suited to their needs.

Overview

Part 1 – Using the workbook

Regaining Control is intended to be used as an individualized program of treatment in either group or one-on-one treatment settings. Chapters are selected with client input according to client needs. Throughout the course of treatment, programs can be adjusted as new information is disclosed. In this section the use of the Client Questionnaire is explained and a hypothetical treatment program is shown for illustration. Part 1 concludes with discussion of the Client Progress Report.

Part 2 – Theory and Practice

Treatment Theory gives a brief overview of some of the more common approaches to sex offender treatment. It proposes an integrative model of treatment based on our emerging knowledge of brain function. The model contrasts the working of the emotional brain with that of the executive brain. Discussion includes the Good Lives model and its use in *Regaining Control*.

Treatment Practice considers the clinician's role in the forensic setting. It discusses the goals and perspectives of various stakeholders in the criminal justice system. The general goals of treatment are discussed along with the client's goals. The therapeutic relationship and client resistance to treatment are addressed. This section concludes with consideration of sexual schema and the limits of change.

Chapter Overview

In this section, a brief overview of workbook chapters is given grouped by treatment cluster.

Forms

The forms used in treatment are listed along with a brief explanation of their use. Forms include the following:

- Chapter Evaluation
- Goals Chart
- My SWOT Plan
- Cycle Analysis
- Statement of Forgiveness

References

A list of selected references is included. This list includes more readily available texts that address topics in *Regaining Control*.

Part 1 - Using the Workbook

Layout and Design

The following chart is listed on page iv of the *Regaining Control* workbook.

Part 1					
		Date			Date
	1 Treatment That Works			12 Why I did it	
	2 Being in Group			13 Needs and Sex	
	3 A Good Life			14 Sex and Healthy Relationships	
	4 What if I'm Innocent?			15 Sexual Beliefs	
	5 Stance Toward Treatment			16 Sex and Relationships	
	6 Forming Goals			17 Rules	
	7 Resources			18 Pessimists and Optimists	
	8 Stages of Change			19 Action Planning	
	9 Life History			20 Planning Success	
	10 My Story			21 Purpose	
	11 Brains and Mental Health			22 Back to the Good Life	

Part 2					
		Date			Date
	23 Emotional Thinking			45 Escaping the Cycle	
	24 Cures for Emotional Thinking			46 Sex Addiction – Beginnings	
	25 Breaking Habits			47 Sex Addiction – Beliefs	
	26 Chains and Cycles			48 Pornography	
	27 Breaking Links			49 Porn Progression	
	28 Where Thoughts Lie			50 Masturbation and Imagination	
	29 Barriers to Change			51 Arousing Curves	
	30 Shame			52 Developing Brains	
	31 Forgiveness			53 Paraphilias	
	32 Sexual Scheming			54 Nature Versus Nurture	
	33 Changing Schemas			55 Disease and Choice	
	34 Imagination			56 Reflex Emotions and EQ	
	35 The Pursuit of Pleasure			57 Learned Emotions and EQ	
	36 Family Cycles and Incest			58 Managing Learn. Emotions Part 1	
	37 The Abuse Survivor's Perspective			59 Managing Learn. Emotions Part 2	
	38 Feelings and Rape			60 EQ and Strong Emotions	
	39 Beliefs and Rape			61 Ethical Reasoning and Empathy	
	40 Setups, Traps, and Controls			62 Fighting the Good Ethical Fight	
	41 Bad Associations			63 Empathy – Feeling for Others	
	42 Sexual Thought Viruses			64 Me in the Mirror	
	43 Sex and Offenses			65 Regaining Trust	
	44 Repeat Offenders			66 Changing Focus	

O = Oral presentation   W = written assignment

Use of the chart will be fully discussed later in this guide. For now, note that Part 1 contains material that is relevant to most clients, therefore, clients will be assigned most, if not all, of these chapters.

Part 2 of the chart shows a range of topics that are assigned according to client need. The use of this section will also be fully discussed later.

As the chart shows, the workbook contains sixty-six chapters. The chapters can be completed sequentially or in the order the clinician and/or client chooses. Part 1 is normally completed first as it serves as foundation for chapters that follow in Part 2.

In my practice, clients were assigned on average between twenty and thirty chapters. Because chapters were assigned during the client's intake, I always advised clients that the assignments were a starting point, and that additional chapters could be assigned as more information became available during treatment. I chose to add chapters only when clearly indicated, as I did not want clients withholding information out of fear that they would be assigned further work.

I also offered to modify client's programs if they showed interest in making presentations on other material they had not been assigned. Modifications could include changing some assignments to written form and adding assignments in which they showed interest. Additional assignments could also be submitted in written form without modifying the client's existing assignments.

Completing Chapters

Each chapter contains questions interspersed within the text. Clients are asked to answer these questions and either submit their answers to the clinician, or to orally present their answers to the group or the clinician. When the client has answered all the questions in the chapter, or completed the chapter in any manner the clinician has approved, they are given credit for the chapter.

Clients can be given the option of discussing the chapter material in a manner other than just answering the questions. The Chapter Presentation worksheet provides an outline that can be used to summarize the main points of the chapter and their application to the client's life.

Evaluating whether a client has adequately demonstrated understanding of a chapter is a judgement call based on a number of factors including: client education, background, fear of public speaking, ability to read, and psychological mindedness, to name a few. Some clients may need considerable help understanding and answering chapter questions. Others are more inclined to skim the surface of the questions and need the encouragement of the group to consider the deeper issues of the chapter.

In cases where clients are illiterate, the therapist may have to walk them through the chapter material and questions. (An audio version of the workbook is available for clients who have difficulty reading.) If clients are simply unable to present to the group, all assignments may be submitted in written form. In general, the approach to assignments should be supportive. As treatment progresses, the client is encouraged to assume a greater degree of responsibility to demonstrate understanding of course material.

Completion Criteria

Clients are entitled to a reasonable estimate of the time they will spend in treatment. Having a more definite treatment framework helps clients avoid unreasonable expectations (Can I complete in a month?) and helps provide motivation to do the work. During the intake process, the clinician gathers client information and selects chapters from the workbook that address their concerns and experience. Once chapters are assigned, clients have an estimate of how long they will be in treatment. Giving the client a timeframe for completion helps them to become more engaged in the process. Client programs may be modified when new information about their history is disclosed during group, their supervising officer reveals violations, or information is disclosed during a polygraph.

Once clients have finished assigned material, their treatment program is complete. Could clients have benefitted from more treatment? Certainly. Some clients may elect to remain in treatment longer by either delaying the completion of their final assignments, or by attending groups after program completion. Most choose to terminate treatment once their program is complete. My goal was that all clients would complete treatment. When I began using the *Regaining Control* workbook, completion rates increased significantly. Clients were less inclined to simply "sit out" their probation time. When presented with the possibility of completing treatment earlier if they worked to complete assignments, most clients saw the benefit of doing the work and graduated from the program.

My clients were treated in the community and met weekly. Some clients also attended individual treatment, but were expected to attend weekly groups as well. Length of treatment varied from between six months and three or more years, depending on the effort they demonstrated. The average time in treatment was about two years.

Modified Treatment Programs

Most clients come to treatment with two or more years of probation to complete. Others begin treatment with six months or less. Clients with shorter probationary periods frequently have committed or pleaded to offenses that were less serious. In some cases, clients may have attended treatment prior to incarceration or following treatment with another provider. Whenever feasible, programs were modified to allow these clients to complete their program in an expedited manner, giving them credit for prior treatment. This can be done by giving them a greater proportion of written assignments.

When is Enough, Enough?

What of those clients who complete the workbook assignments but who clearly do not seem to have benefitted? It is clear that no amount of psychological support will induce some clients to change. *Regaining Control* accepts that there are limits to brain change. In those cases, it was my practice to "graduate" a client (if they had satisfactorily completed all assignments and demonstrated understanding of the material). Program completion, after all, is not a guarantee clients will not repeat past mistakes. It is simply a statement that they have demonstrated understanding of treatment concepts. If in the course of a two-year treatment program a client shows no willingness to change, it is doubtful that additional time in treatment will make much difference. As clinicians we recognize that the struggle between the emotional and executive brains is a life-long one. Some clients simply are unwilling or unable to change despite our best efforts.

8

Client Programs

Client Questionnaire

The Client Questionnaire can be used to determine the client's treatment focus areas. Clients may complete the form on their own or with their treatment provider. Clients are encouraged to complete the questionnaire as truthfully as possible. Most clients want to reduce their time in treatment, and therefore may attempt to answer these questions in a way that would shorten their program. Trying to "fool the test" is generally not productive. It does not shorten treatment time significantly and can keep the client from benefitting fully from the treatment experience.

It should be noted that a client's program should not be based solely on their answers to these questions. The client's program is dynamic. Treatment providers may choose to add or remove assignments as treatment progresses, based on the client's level of participation and future disclosures.

As the clinician becomes familiar with the material in *Regaining Control,* an oral interview covering the clusters discussed below, can be substituted.

The scoring sheet with instructions is included following the questionnaire.

The publisher's website contains additional tools to assist with setting up and tracking client programs. See WritePsych.com for details.

Client Questionnaire

☐ Agree ☐ Disagree 1. I have never been in sex offender treatment before.

☐ Agree ☐ Disagree 2. I think treatment is a waste of time.

☐ Agree ☐ Disagree 3. I worry about being in treatment.

☐ Agree ☐ Disagree 4. I have had negative experiences in prior treatment.

☐ Agree ☐ Disagree 5. I don't think I need treatment.

☐ Agree ☐ Disagree 6. I have a hard time accomplishing challenging goals.

☐ Agree ☐ Disagree 7. I don't have the support I need to accomplish my goals.

☐ Agree ☐ Disagree 8. I usually don't accomplish my goals.

☐ Agree ☐ Disagree 9. People don't see me as a successful person.

☐ Agree ☐ Disagree 10. I frequently break the rules.

☐ Agree ☐ Disagree 11. I have gotten into trouble more than most.

☐ Agree ☐ Disagree 12. I think rules are often unreasonable.

☐ Agree ☐ Disagree 13. I often struggle to know what is right and wrong.

☐ Agree ☐ Disagree 14. I don't have a clear idea of what I would like to accomplish in life.

☐ Agree ☐ Disagree 15. I don't think I can have a satisfying life.

☐ Agree ☐ Disagree 16. I don't know what my purpose in life is.

☐ Agree ☐ Disagree 17. I don't know why I acted in a way that got me into trouble.

☐ Agree ☐ Disagree 18. I was not the only one responsible for my offense.

☐ Agree ☐ Disagree 19. If I could do it over again, I would do the same thing that got me in trouble.

☐ Agree ☐ Disagree 20. I have stronger needs related to sex than most.

☐ Agree ☐ Disagree 21. Sex one of my most important needs.

☐ Agree ☐ Disagree 22. I have a history of mental health problems.

☐ Agree ☐ Disagree 23. I have thoughts I can't get out of my head.

☐ Agree ☐ Disagree 24. I sometimes wonder why I do things I know are wrong.

☐ Agree ☐ Disagree 25. I am taking medications for a mental health condition.

☐ Agree ☐ Disagree 26. I didn't do what I was accused of.

☐ Agree ☐ Disagree 27. Someone else was mostly responsible for me getting charged with my crime.

☐ Agree ☐ Disagree 28. I feel like the system has treated me unfairly.

☐ Agree ☐ Disagree 29. I have committed or been charged with more than one sex offense.

☐ Agree ☐ Disagree 30. I have been accused of a similar offense occurring on several occasions.

☐ Agree ☐ Disagree 31. I have stopped a problem sexual behavior but later repeated it again.

☐ Agree ☐ Disagree 32. I sometimes repeat negative behaviors without knowing why.

☐ Agree ☐ Disagree 33. I am sexually attracted to things that people don't understand.

☐ Agree ☐ Disagree 34. I have gotten into trouble for doing sexual things that aren't considered normal.

☐ Agree ☐ Disagree 35. I sometimes struggle with troubling sexual thoughts or fantasies.

☐ Agree ☐ Disagree 36. I am confused about how I feel about sex.

☐ Agree ☐ Disagree 37. I find it difficult to make new friends.

Client Questionnaire

☐ Agree ☐ Disagree 38. People do not understand me.

☐ Agree ☐ Disagree 39. Sex a very important part of a good relationship.

☐ Agree ☐ Disagree 40. People sometimes complain that I don't understand them.

☐ Agree ☐ Disagree 41. If someone loves you, they should be willing to have sex with you.

☐ Agree ☐ Disagree 42. I used to view pornography regularly.

☐ Agree ☐ Disagree 43. My use of pornography has caused problems for me.

☐ Agree ☐ Disagree 44. I find it hard to stop viewing pornography.

☐ Agree ☐ Disagree 45. I have lied about, or hidden, my use of pornography.

☐ Agree ☐ Disagree 46. I sometimes experience strong feelings that get in the way of doing what is right.

☐ Agree ☐ Disagree 47. I see my crime very differently than others.

☐ Agree ☐ Disagree 48. I often go with my feelings rather than thinking things through.

☐ Agree ☐ Disagree 49. I have done things when I was sexually aroused that I later regretted.

☐ Agree ☐ Disagree 50. I feel overwhelming shame and guilt about my offense.

☐ Agree ☐ Disagree 51. I don't think I should be forgiven for what I did.

☐ Agree ☐ Disagree 52. I think my crime was so bad that I should never experience a good life.

☐ Agree ☐ Disagree 53. My offense involved sex with a relative.

☐ Agree ☐ Disagree 54. I or others in my family were victims of incest (sex with a relative).

☐ Agree ☐ Disagree 55. My offense involved using force to get someone to do what I wanted.

☐ Agree ☐ Disagree 56. I sometimes have to force partners to do what I want sexually.

☐ Agree ☐ Disagree 57. I think some people owe me sex.

☐ Agree ☐ Disagree 58. Sexual partners sometimes resist but really want to have sex.

☐ Agree ☐ Disagree 59. I think about sex more than most people do.

☐ Agree ☐ Disagree 60. Sex is a very important need in my life.

☐ Agree ☐ Disagree 61. My sexual behaviors have gotten me into trouble.

☐ Agree ☐ Disagree 62 I engage in sexual behaviors more often than I would like to.

☐ Agree ☐ Disagree 63. Sometimes I engage in risky or dangerous sexual behaviors.

☐ Agree ☐ Disagree 64. I have a hard time controlling my feelings.

☐ Agree ☐ Disagree 65. I get angry often or can't control my anger.

☐ Agree ☐ Disagree 66. I struggle with depression, anxiety, fear, or other negative feelings.

☐ Agree ☐ Disagree 67. My feelings get in the way of making positive choices.

☐ Agree ☐ Disagree 68. I find it hard to understand other people.

☐ Agree ☐ Disagree 69. I wonder why people get upset with me.

☐ Agree ☐ Disagree 70. It is sometimes okay to hurt someone if they get in my way.

☐ Agree ☐ Disagree 71. Other people often get in the way of getting what I want.

☐ Agree ☐ Disagree 72. I see myself in a negative way.

☐ Agree ☐ Disagree 73. Sometimes I feel broken or defective.

☐ Agree ☐ Disagree 74. I don't think I can become a better person.

Client Questionnaire

☐ Agree ☐ Disagree 75. I consider myself superior to others.

☐ Agree ☐ Disagree 76. I spend more time than most imagining sexual things.

☐ Agree ☐ Disagree 77. My fantasies are sometimes unusual or disturbing.

☐ Agree ☐ Disagree 78. Sometimes I think about unhealthy or dangerous things to make me feel better.

Client Questionnaire Score Sheet

Questions	Total Agree Answers	Cluster	Workbook chapters
1		Prior Treatment	1, 2
2, 3, 4, 5		Treatment View	5, 8, 18
6, 7, 8, 9		Goals	6, 7, 19, 20
10, 11, 12, 13		Rules	17
14, 15, 16		Good Life	3, 21, 22
17, 18, 19, 20, 21		Background	9, 10, 12, 13
22, 23, 24, 25		Mental Health	11
26, 27, 28		Denial/Innocence	4
29, 30, 31, 32		Repetition	25, 26, 27, 44, 45
33, 34, 35, 36		Schema	32, 33, 41, 43, 52, 53, 54, 55
37, 38,3 9, 40, 41		Relationships	14, 15, 16
42, 43, 44, 45		Pornography	48, 49, 50
46, 47, 48, 49		Cognitive Distortions	23, 24, 28, 42, 51
50, 51, 52		Shame	29, 30, 31,
53, 54		Incest	36, 37
55, 56, 57, 58		Rape	38, 39, 40
59, 60, 61, 62, 63		Sex Addiction	46, 47
64, 65, 66, 67		Emotions	56,5 7, 58, 59, 60
68, 69, 70, 71		Empathy	61, 62, 63, 65
72, 73, 74, 75		Self-Image	64, 66
76, 77, 78		Fantasy	34, 35

To score the questionnaire, add up the total "Agree" answers to the questions listed in the "Questions" column. Mark the total in the column titled "Total Agree Answers". If the score is two or more, then complete the workbook chapters listed in the "Workbook Chapters" column. (Since there is only one question in the first row for the Prior Treatment cluster, only 1 Agree answer is needed to assign chapters 1 and 2.)

Example:

Questions	Total Agree Answers	Cluster	Workbook chapters
1	1	Prior Treatment	1, 2
2, 3, 4, 5	3	Treatment View	5, 8, 18
6, 7, 8, 9	1	Goals	None - or as needed

In this example, the client scored 1 Agree answer for question 1, 3 Agree answers for questions 2-5, and 1 Agree answer for questions 6-9. This person would complete chapters 1, 2, 5, 8, and 18. Chapters 6,7,19, and 20 are not required but may be considered since the client has only one Agree answer in this row. Additional chapters may be assigned as the client progresses in treatment.

Treatment Program Example

Regaining Control is designed to assist the treatment provider in creating a therapy program tailored to meet the individual client's needs. It uses clusters of topics which focus on target areas. The clusters are shown below followed by a brief description and the workbook chapters which address them:

Treatment Clusters

Cluster	Target Area	Workbook Chapters
Prior Treatment	Client has not been in treatment for a sexual offense before	1, 2
Treatment View	Client has a negative view of treatment	5, 8, 18
Goals	Client struggles to define and accomplish goals	6, 7, 19, 20
Rules	Client has a history of breaking rules or laws	17
Good Life	Client lacks view of a healthy, fulfilling life	3, 21, 22
Background	Client's life history and its relation to offense and other concerns	9, 10, 12, 13
Mental Health	Client has mental health issues – diagnosed or undiagnosed	11
Denial/Innocence	Client has committed an offense which he denies or minimizes	4
Repetition	Client has a history of multiple offenses	25, 26, 27, 44, 45
Schema	Client shows distortions of sexual interest (paraphilias)	32, 33, 41, 43, 52, 53, 54, 55
Relationships	Client struggles to establish and maintain healthy relationships	14, 15, 16
Pornography	Client has history of problematic pornography use	48, 49, 50
Cognitive Distortions	Client uses thought processes in ways that harm self or others	23, 24, 28, 42, 51
Shame	Client lacks ability or interest to change due to deep shame	29, 30, 31,
Fantasy	Client engages in extensive sexual fantasy that interferes with life	34, 35
Incest	Client or family members have experienced or perpetrated incest	36, 37
Rape	Client used force or coercion to overcome victim resistance	38, 39, 40
Sex Addiction	Client shows significant compulsive behaviors related to sex	46, 47
Emotions	Client struggles to manage strong emotions	56, 57, 58, 59, 60
Empathy	Client shows lessened ability to understand and feel for others	61, 62, 63, 65
Self-Image	Client has poor self-image	64, 66

Treatment providers may use the treatment clusters as a guide or select chapters individually for clients. Clients are encouraged to participate in chapter selection as well.

Regaining Control is divided into two parts. Part 1 addresses treatment topics common to most clients. In most cases, clients will complete all of these chapters. Part 2 addresses specific client issues. These should be assigned based on the client's responses to the Client Survey, client background material, and their interactions with the treatment provider and group. Additional chapters may be assigned as indicated during the course of treatment. The example below shows part of the form completed for a hypothetical client. The box to the left of the chapter indicates chapters which have been assigned to the client, and how the client is to complete the chapter. When the chapter is completed, the date of completion can be entered into the Date box to the right of the chapter title

Assignment Completion and Presentations

Clients complete assignments by submitting written responses to chapter questions or through oral presentations summarizing chapter material to their treatment group or therapist. In the authors' program, all clients participated in group. All group members make oral presentations (marked "O" in the example) or submit written responses (marked "W" in the example) to workbook material in both parts of the workbook. During each group, two clients presented their material for half an hour. Clients were assigned to make presentations on a rotating basis. Depending on the size of the group (usually between sex and ten), clients expected to present their material every three to five weeks. Clients were encouraged to cover one chapter during each presentation. Written material was reviewed then checked off as completed or (rarely) returned back to the client for further work.

Sample Treatment Program (only part of the form is shown)

Part 1					
		Date			Date
	1 Treatment That Works		O	12 Why I did it	
	2. Being in Group		O	13 Needs and Sex	
O	3. A Good Life	1/1/18	O	14 Sex and Healthy Relationships	
O	4. What if I'm Innocent?	2/2/18	O	15 Sexual Beliefs	
O	5. Stance Toward Treatment		O	16 Sex and Relationships	
O	6. Forming Goals		O	17 Rules	
O	7. Resources		O	18 Pessimists and Optimists	
O	8. Stages of Change		O	19 Action Planning	
O	9 Life History		O	20 Planning Success	
O	10 My Story		O	21 Purpose	
O	11 Brains and Mental Health		O	22 Back to the Good Life	
Part 2					
		Date			Date
W	23 Emotional Thinking	1/14/18	O	45 Escaping the Cycle	
O	24 Cures for Emotional Thinking			46 Sex Addiction – Beginnings	
W	25 Breaking Habits			47 Sex Addiction – Beliefs	

In this example, written assignments are indicated by a "W" in the column left of the chapter. Oral presentations are indicated with an "O" in this column. The client in this example has been in treatment before, and therefore he is not assigned chapters 1 and 2. Most clients entering treatment are assigned most chapters in Part 1. This example also shows the client has been assigned chapters in Part 2 (only partially shown) which address emotional thinking, breaking habits, and pornography. Three chapters have been completed as indicated by the dates in the "Date" boxes. In this case, the client made an oral presentation to group on 1/1/18, submitted a written assignment on 1/14/18, then made another oral presentation on 2/2/18. The client is not required to study chapters not marked "O" or "W" in the boxes preceding the chapter number. When all marked chapters have been completed, the client has completed the assigned material in the workbook and their treatment program is complete.

The full Client Treatment Program form is shown on the next page.

See the publisher's website for instructional videos on the use of the workbook. The Regaining Control Database can also be downloaded from the publisher's site. It can be used to set up client programs and track client progress in treatment. Visit WritePsych.com for additional resources.

Client Treatment Program

Client Name:____   Date:_____________________________

Evaluator Name:____

Part 1				
		Date		Date
	1 Treatment That Works		12 Why I did it	
	2. Being in Group		13 Needs and Sex	
	3. A Good Life		14 Sex and Healthy Relationships	
	4. What if I'm Innocent?		15 Sexual Beliefs	
	5. Stance Toward Treatment		16 Sex and Relationships	
	6. Forming Goals		17 Rules	
	7. Resources		18 Pessimists and Optimists	
	8. Stages of Change		19 Action Planning	
	9. Life History		20 Planning Success	
	10 My Story		21 Purpose	
	11 Brains and Mental Health		22 Back to the Good Life	

Part 2				
		Date		Date
	23 Emotional Thinking		45 Escaping the Cycle	
	24 Cures for Emotional Thinking		46 Sex Addiction – Beginnings	
	25 Breaking Habits		47 Sex Addiction – Beliefs	
	26 Chains and Cycles		48 Pornography	
	27 Breaking Links		49 Porn Progression	
	28 Where Thoughts Lie		50 Masturbation and Imagination	
	29 Barriers to Change		51 Arousing Curves	
	30 Shame		52 Developing Brains	
	31 Forgiveness		53 Paraphilias	
	32 Sexual Scheming		54 Nature Versus Nurture	
	33 Changing Schemas		55 Disease and Choice	
	34 Imagination		56 Reflex Emotions and EQ	
	35 The Pursuit of Pleasure		57 Learned Emotions and EQ	
	36 Family Cycles and Incest		58 Managing Learn. Emotions Part 1	
	37 The Abuse Survivor's Perspective		59 Managing Learn. Emotions Part 2	
	38 Feelings and Rape		60 EQ and Strong Emotions	
	39 Beliefs and Rape		61 Ethical Reasoning and Empathy	
	40 Setups, Traps, and Controls		62 Fighting the Good Ethical Fight	
	41 Bad Associations		63 Empathy – Feeling for Others	
	42 Sexual Thought Viruses		64 Me in the Mirror	
	43 Sex and Offenses		65 Regaining Trust	
	44 Repeat Offenders		66 Changing Focus	

O = Oral presentation   W = written assignment

Client Progress Report

The Client Progress Report form is used to periodically assess client progress in treatment. It is completed by the treatment provider in partnership with the client, and, when feasible, others who are part of the client's program such as parole/probation officers and other treatment providers. A blank form is shown on the next page. Additional forms are available for download on the publisher's website.

Client Progress Report

Name: _______________________________ **Period:**___________________ **Date:** ___________

Stage of Change: ☐ Pre-contemplation ☐ Contemplation ☐ Preparation ☐ Action ☐ Maintenance

Goal Accomplishment: ☐ Accomplishes healthy goals ☐ Makes effective plans to reach goals ☐ Shows little or no progress toward accomplishing goals ☐ Has not identified goals

Cognitions: ☐ Corrects problem thinking ☐ Recognizes problem thinking but has not taken action to correct it ☐ Denies or minimizes problem thinking

Emotional Regulation: ☐ Manages emotions consistently ☐ Meets emotional needs in healthy ways ☐ Understands influence of emotions on thinking and behavior ☐ Frequently allows emotions to negatively influence thinking and behavior ☐ Denies need to manage emotions

Treatment Participation – Group/Individual: ☐ Actively participates ☐ Supports other group members ☐ Provides helpful feedback ☐ Does not participate in group ☐ Disrupts group process ☐ Creates conflict with other group members ☐ Is argumentative and resists feedback

Treatment Participation – Program: ☐ Maintains good attendance ☐ Adheres to treatment contract or rules ☐ Is current on financial obligations ☐ Is out of compliance with treatment contract

Assignment Progress: ☐ Shows good understanding of course concepts ☐ Makes well prepared presentations ☐ Applies course concepts to life ☐ Is not completing assignments as scheduled ☐ Refuses to complete assignments

Completion of Treatment: ☐ Has satisfied treatment requirements ☐ Is on pace to complete treatment in timely manner ☐ Is progressing inconsistently through treatment material ☐ Is progressing at a much slower pace than expected ☐ Is not making progress toward completing treatment program

Risk Management:
☐ Assumes responsibility for offense
☐ Does not engage in behaviors that could contribute to future offenses
☐ Does not indicate attitudes supportive of sexual offending
☐ Indicates desire to refrain from deviant or harmful sexual behaviors
☐ Uses effective strategies to manage potentially harmful sexual motivations and acts
☐ Abides by laws, conditions of release, and treatment contract
☐ Demonstrates attitudes supportive of rule adherence

ASSESSMENTS

Client was evaluated using ____and received a rating of _______________________ indicating a _______________________ level of need/risk.

Prepared by: ___________________________________ Date: ___________________

One or more checkboxes may be marked by the evaluator for each area of focus. The areas of focus are shown below with brief explanations stating when the boxes should be checked.

Stages of Change

- Pre-contemplation – client sees no need to change and denies problem thoughts, feelings, or behaviors.
- Contemplation – client is aware of problem thoughts, feelings, and behaviors, and is considering the need to change.
- Preparation – client is aware of need to change and is beginning to put things in place to make change happen.
- Action – client is actively pursuing change as shown in his self-report, workbook assignments, and reports by others who have contact with the client.
- Maintenance – client demonstrates consistent, long-term, meaningful changes in problem behaviors and is able to effectively address lapses into negative behaviors.

Goal Accomplishment

- Accomplishes healthy goals – client has established and achieved positive goals during treatment.
- Makes effective plans to reach goals – client is able to formulate reasonable plans to accomplish goals though they may have not been completed yet.
- Shows little or no progress toward accomplishing goals – client has not established effective goals nor have they formulated effective strategies to accomplish them.
- Has not identified goals – client has not identified goals or strategies to accomplish them and demonstrates unwillingness to progress in this area.

Cognitions

- Corrects problem thinking – client has demonstrated ability to identify problem thinking and has made effective changes to problem thinking.
- Recognizes problem thinking but has not taken action to correct it – though the client is able to identify problem thinking, they choose not to correct it.
- Denies or minimizes problem thinking – client is unwilling or unable to identify and correct problem thinking.

Emotional Regulation

- Manages emotions consistently – client shows ability to manage strong emotions in personal life and during group or individual sessions.
- Meets emotional needs in healthy ways – client understands their emotional needs and finds positive ways to express and manage them.
- Understands influence of emotions on thinking and behavior – client is able to identify the ways emotions influence their thinking and behaviors but is inconsistent managing emotions.

- Frequently allows emotions to negatively influence thinking and behavior – client shows little control over negative emotions and acts out in negative ways in his personal life or treatment setting.
- Denies need to manage emotions – client denies their need to exercise emotional regulation even though client's experience indicates deficits in this area.

Treatment Participation – Group/Individual

- Actively participates – client actively works to understand communications by others in the treatment setting and tailors their discussion to meet the needs of the group.
- Supports other group members – client works to understand others' perspectives and offers empathic support to other members.
- Provides helpful feedback – client offers helpful suggestions, asks thoughtful questions, and provides encouragement to others in the treatment setting.
- Does not participate in group – client does not attend to discussion or show interest in group process.
- Disrupts group process – client makes comments intended to disrupt or engages in conduct that is threatening, intimidating, or otherwise detracts from group process.
- Creates conflict with other group members – client intentionally pits group members against each other, spreads rumors, or discredits other members without cause.
- Is argumentative or fails to consider feedback – client regularly disputes the relevance of feedback offered to him or takes opposing views for the sake of arguing.

Treatment Participation – Program

- Maintains good attendance – client attends group or treatment sessions as scheduled or notifies provider of absences as required in treatment contract or rules.
- Adheres to treatment contract or rules – client abides by treatment rules specified by their treatment provider.
- Is current on financial obligations – client is current on treatment related costs or has made arrangements with provider to address these expenses.
- Is out of compliance with treatment – client is not adhering to his treatment contract or rules and has shown little or no effort to be in compliance.

Assignment Progress

- Shows good understanding of course concepts – client demonstrates understanding of course principles and their application to their life.
- Makes well prepared presentations – client studies workbook material and presents what he has learned in an effective manner.
- Applies course concepts to life – client understands how treatment material is relevant to his life and applies treatment concepts on a consistent basis.
- Is not completing assignments as scheduled – client shows significant delay in completing course work.

- Refuses to complete assignments – client refuses to complete assignments because they believe the course material does not apply, though the client's history and treatment interactions indicate otherwise.

Completion of Treatment

- Has satisfied treatment requirements – client has met treatment conditions as outlined in their program.
- Is on pace to complete treatment in timely manner – client is progressing at an appropriate pace and anticipates completing treatment.
- Is progressing inconsistently through treatment material – client's progress shows gaps such as frequent absences, or frequently has not completed assignments.
- Is progressing at much slower pace than expected – client is making progress but at a significantly slower pace than expected given the client's program.
- Is not making progress – client is not making progress through course material.

Risk Management

- Assumes responsibility for offense – client does not blame others, minimize, deny, or use other defenses to avoid responsibility for actions.
- Does not engage in behaviors that could contribute to future offenses – client is no longer engaged in behaviors associated with their offense and is involved in activities supportive of an offense-free lifestyle.
- Does not indicate attitudes supportive of sexual offending – client views sexual offenses as harmful and understands the negative effects of such behavior on self and others.
- Indicates desire to refrain from deviant or harmful sexual behaviors – client understands the nature of harmful or deviant sexual behavior and is committed to refraining from such behaviors.
- Uses effective strategies to manage potentially harmful sexual motivations and acts – client is employing effective strategies to manage potentially harmful sexual urges and refrains from acting on these urges.
- Abides by laws, conditions of release, and treatment contract/rules – client consistently adheres to treatment and supervision rules or acknowledges violations and uses appropriate strategies to avoid violations in the future.
- Demonstrates attitudes supportive of rule adherence – client indicates a desire to follow treatment or supervision rules and indicates intent to abide by them in the future, if a violation occurs.

Assessments

A variety of assessments may also be used to gauge the client's progress in treatment or level of risk. If an assessment is used as part of the evaluation, it should be listed in the space provided at the bottom of the form.

Part 2 - Theory and Practice

Treatment Theory

The Addiction Treatment Model

The addiction treatment model views client behaviors supportive of drug abuse as the result of disease. The view holds that clients act in ways they otherwise would not under the compulsions created by disease. Treatment is a vehicle to address the physiological and emotional/cognitive processes that foster ongoing drug abuse. Clients are taught to avoid situations where triggers to abuse drugs may be present. They also learn to manage cognitions that lead to abuse such as minimizing, rationalizing, justifying, and so on. With continued abuse, addicts experience cravings and alterations in behavior that facilitate their addictive lifestyle. Abuse leads to disease, and disease leads to further abuse.

Sex offenders seem to fit this model in significant ways. They often describe engaging in behaviors that are unwanted, repeated, and self-destructive. They may even experience compulsions to act out, even though they find their behavior reprehensible. The damage they have suffered in their own lives or created in the lives of others, for which they often experience remorse, suggests that clients are suffering from an illness. The need to repeatedly engage in sexual activity to satisfy cravings or to cope with stressors, also suggests parallels.

Therapies that approach sexual abuse through relapse prevention—avoidance and cognitive restructuring—follow the addiction treatment model. Many clients find this approach a good fit for their experience. Clients who say their offense was part of an ongoing pattern of worsening behavior meant to satisfy sexual compulsions, relate to this model. It could be said that behaviors that satisfied sexual cravings was their drug of choice. Clients who experienced addiction to pornography are a good example of the addiction model and are often labelled "pornography addicts." They suffer unwanted side-effects and in some cases, develop such a preference for pornography that their sexual experience with others suffers.

While the addiction model fits some clients, many clients' offense history tells a different tale. They say that their offense was a singular instance or part of only a few instances where they acted out under a set of unique circumstances. Such circumstances often include relationship difficulties with a significant other, a period of mental illness (depression, mania, etc.), heightened life stressors, perceived grievances, lack of validation, and the opportunity afforded by the victim's presence. Once these circumstances were resolved, the impulses to act out sexually ceased or diminished significantly. These clients might be compared to persons who abused drugs to cope with negative circumstances, then stopped using on their own. These clients, while not being classified as addicts, could benefit from working on coping skills to address the contributors to their offense. In the drug treatment field, they benefit from relapse prevention training.

While the addiction treatment model offers many sound interventions, it may not address other related issues that are unique to sex offenders. Avoidance of "triggers" may not adequately address relational, social, and cognitive contributors to their offense.

Conditioning

Treatment may also include the use of conditioning by pairing aversive stimuli with the thoughts and behaviors to be extinguished (sniffing ammonia when viewing or wanting to view pornography, for example). Some providers may also use rewards to shape thoughts and behaviors (imagining appropriate sexual partners during masturbation). The treatment setting itself can be viewed as an extension of conditioning. A supportive group environment where offenders share their stories can foster further disclosures. Group reinforcement may help a client to appreciate the negative impacts of their behavior on others.

Incarceration can also be viewed as a conditioning approach. Many clients say avoiding incarceration is their primary motivation not to repeat past offenses. For these clients, memories of their experience in custody provide motivation to do the work of treatment. Some clients, however, are so traumatized by the experience, they simply attempt to avoid addressing it. They may struggle to consider the causes of their actions—their thoughts and feelings—preferring to simply put the past behind them.

While conditioning can be an effective part of the learning process, it is often not sufficient to help clients act appropriately. Clients who know better, don't necessarily do better.

Cognitive Behavioral Therapy

Regaining Control uses a cognitive-behavioral approach. It examines the interplay between thoughts, feelings, and behaviors. It attempts to address conflicts between feelings and thoughts that give rise to unwanted behaviors. Offenders often view their offenses as contrary to their beliefs about what is acceptable conduct. Treatment explores the client's beliefs related to ethical behavior. *Regaining Control* examines the nature of the inner conflict that leads to clients acting out.

Emotional and Executive Brain Conflict

The workbook's approach is based on the premise that two systems are responsible for behavior—the "emotional brain" (limbic system) and the "executive brain" (pre-frontal lobes and related areas). While it is recognized that this "two-brain" model is a vastly oversimplified explanation on a neuro-cognitive level, it is sufficient to explain the experience most client's describe surrounding their offense.

In this approach, clients learn to identify emotions and their influence on cognition. They learn to recognize when emotions are exerting their effect in sexual and non-sexual settings. *Regaining Control* considers the physiology of sex to be perhaps the most dramatic example of the influence of feelings on thinking. Clients also learn to recognize distortions in thought (thinking errors) that often serve to justify emotionally induced behavior.

The tug-o-war between the emotional and executive brains is viewed as a part of the human experience. Clients are taught that by strengthening the use of the executive brain, they can gain greater control over the emotions that have contributed to harmful behavior in the past.

The Good Lives Model

Perhaps the highest order of executive function is the formation of long-term goals and strategies to accomplish them. This requires evaluation of many possible futures and the actions needed to accomplish them. Most clients want a good life. Most believe it is still possible to have one. Many have not spent much time actually planning to achieve one. Many offenders have a history of impulsivity with many partially constructed goals and little planning to accomplish them. Clients may say they are motivated to avoid past mistakes, but have given little thought to how they will achieve this.

The Good Lives Model seeks to add incentive by helping clients clarify their notions of what a good life is. Once a client has a clear vision of their positive future, treatment then proceeds to reinforce this future and the thoughts, feelings, and behaviors that are most likely to accomplish it. Few offenders want to return to jail or prison. Most want to lead productive lives, free of supervision. Most want to experience meaningful relationships. Many hope to reconcile with estranged spouses, children, friends, and community groups. Reinforcing the need to manage emotional and cognitive processes becomes the key to achieving these goals.

Clients learn that a good life is often difficult to achieve, and thus, requires the exercise of executive control. Throughout treatment, clients work toward greater executive control as they learn to manage the negative emotions and thinking that might trigger relapse into old behaviors.

Neuroscience and the Nature of Being Human

Regaining Control attempts to incorporate findings from cognitive science. The workbook contrasts the differences between the limbic system (emotional brain) and the prefrontal cortex (executive brain). It is recognized that neuroscience has much more to learn about the interplay between the systems of the brain. Furthermore, it is also recognized that this demarcation of the brain into two competing systems is vastly simplified. Even so, this two competing systems approach does provide a useful way to discuss the client experience. The two systems are conceived as follows.

Emotional Brain

The primary function of the emotional brain is to assess and formulate responses to stimuli. Its function is to store non-verbal reactions to events, people, and circumstances to guide conduct. It does so at both a conscious and unconscious level. Clients may have strong reactions to stimuli without knowing why. Some of these reactions may be based in experiences clients had when they were too young to describe verbally what had occurred. The emotional brain's contribution is to provide a consistent, immediate response to perceptions. *Regaining Control* considers the fight, flight, or freeze emotions as examples of these, though the emotional brain has many more subtle influences which also affect cognition. The emotional brain influences cognitions in many ways. It shapes memories, filters sensory data, and gives meaning to experiences, to name a few.

Executive Brain

In *Regaining Control,* the executive brain's functions include: planning for the future, evaluating strategies to accomplish goals, considering consequences, evaluating thoughts and modifying them to adhere more closely to reality, and regulating emotions. The executive brain's task of regulating the emotional brain is viewed as the key to client success. During treatment, clients begin to understand the differences in brain function and the resulting conflict that can ensue. They often find that this struggle of two brains fits their experience. They say that at the time of their offense, they yielded control from the executive brain to the emotional brain.

To what degree executive control can be learned or strengthened among adult offenders is a question that deserves further study. Interestingly, some clients say that following their offense, they "grew up." By this they mean, they were less selfish and more considerate of the effects of their actions on others. Maturity can be described as the process by which greater control is transitioned from the emotional brain to the executive brain.

Maturation

Areas of the brain mature at different times. The infant comes into the world with a fully formed limbic system. It isn't until an individual is in their middle twenties that the neural pathways connecting the prefrontal cortex to the lower brain centers are fully myelinated. This is viewed by some as the physiological basis for much of the poor decision making witnessed in youth. The teen years seem to supercharge the limbic system while the still-developing higher thinking centers struggle to manage emotions. Furthermore, the neural pathways between the emotional and executive brains are not equal. Pathways from the limbic system to the frontal lobes are more robustly formed than those leading the reverse direction. Thus, the emotional brain more strongly influences executive function.

Neuroplasticity suggests that brain connections can be strengthened. It remains to be seen to what degree the connections that regulate emotions can be modified. *Regaining Control* assumes that clients can strengthen the connections devoted to regulating emotions. Sexual offenses are viewed as the consequence of underutilized or underdeveloped pathways between the executive and emotional brains. Treatment is designed to help clients develop executive control over emotional impulses by exercising these pathways. This view helps to remove the focus of treatment from shame and guilt to learning. Clients still feel negative emotions like shame and remorse, but they find hope in shifting to the work of treatment from the emotional brain (negative feelings) to the executive (planning to avoid problem behavior in the future and achieving positive goals). Some clients describe the process as "growing up."

Sex and Sex Offender Treatment

The differences between the emotional and executive brains is perhaps seen no more dramatically than in the experience of sex. In today's culture, individuals with little executive control are particularly vulnerable. Our society continues to debate about which approach to sex education, if any, is most effective. The goals of education are also unclear. Many clients say they received little sex education and what they did receive was of limited value. Sexual education often comes through the internet or friends. Earliest sex education for many youths essentially consists of exploring what is available online.

Regaining Control assumes that people have a range of sexual interests that influence how sexuality is expressed. For most heterosexual males, this includes viewing pornography depicting women in sexual acts. Though men may also be shown, they are not the center of focus, but rather are a type of surrogate for the viewer. These preferences are the expression of the person's "schema." Schema show some variability for the individual, but the individual retains preferences and may seek stimuli that most closely match their preferences. The plethora of online sites devoted to specific types of pornography may speak to the individual's attempts to find an exact fit for what is most sexually arousing.

It is also a premise of the workbook that the individual's schema is the product of genetics and environment—nature and nurture. Inheritance may create a more variable schema for some clients. This may be shown by broader interests and exploration of online stimuli. Some clients seem to drift further and further away from what would be considered normal. Others may explore to a lesser extent and have a negative or mixed reaction to stimuli outside their schema. Therefore, sexual schema serve both to direct the person's attention to some stimuli while averting it from others.

But what of clients who say their offense was not supported by their beliefs or sexual preferences? *Regaining Control* affirms that clients may act out in ways that are in conflict with their values when sexual impulses overwhelm executive function. Post-offense, most clients believe their actions were wrong. Their feelings of guilt and shame surface after the fact. It should be noted, that their offense usually has parallels with their sexual schema. Men who show a strong preference for women, typically offend against females. Pedophiles are not likely to offend against adults. Clients whose schema is more flexible, may demonstrate a greater range of offending behavior.

Regaining Control attempts to address the range of sexual attitudes and beliefs that could lead to offending behavior. Most clients agree with the boundaries of healthy sex—that sex should be consensual, between adults, and pursued in a way that decreases the spread of disease or unwanted pregnancy. In treatment, client's sexual schemas are identified, as well as their impact on the client's choices. Through discussion of the client's sexual experience, beliefs, and attitudes, treatment brings sex back under the purview of the executive brain. Clients go beyond the feelings of sex to consider its consequences.

It is recognized that some clients' sexual schema biases them toward illegal or harmful sexual behavior. Furthermore, these clients' schema are not likely to change. Therefore, all that can be achieved in treatment is for the client to develop the skills to refrain from acting out on their schema in a manner that violates the law and harms others. *Regaining Control* encourages clients to develop executive control over these interests.

Treatment Practice

Treatment in the Legal Setting

Treatment of forensic clients takes place within two contexts. In the corrections context, offenders are viewed as being responsible for their behavior. Their offenses are seen as the product of intentional and informed action. They are culpable by virtue of the fact that they knew or should have known that their actions were in violation of the law.

In the treatment context, clients are seen to be, to some degree, the victim of their own impulses. The rationale offenders offer to justify their conduct are addressed during treatment. In my experience, most offenders acknowledge that their actions are morally and legally indefensible. Additionally, clients often express remorse when confronted with their actions. They often say they acted out against their own best judgment.

The legal and therapeutic contexts can be viewed as complimentary approaches designed to alter client behavior. They can be viewed as a kind of "good cop, bad cop" approach. The challenges of working in this environment are discussed below.

The Supervision Alliance

Sex offender treatment providers practice within a challenging environment. Clinicians stand at the crossroads of many stakeholders. The courts, law enforcement, and corrections supervisors are tasked with primarily ensuring that offenders do not reoffend. To this end, they impose strict requirements for client conduct. Typically these restrictions include prohibitions against drug/alcohol use, visiting adult entertainment establishments, use of the internet and cell phones, where clients can work, what types of jobs they can hold, whether they can have contact with juveniles and family members, where they can travel, where they can live, and a host of other restrictions thought to be relevant to their offense.

This emphasis on crime prevention often results in clients resenting the rules that seem to hinder them from getting on with their lives. Their most important goals—reuniting with family members, securing better living conditions, finding satisfying work—may be thwarted by the conditions of their release. Some offenders come to believe that their community supervisors are more focused on catching them doing wrong than supporting them in doing what is right. Offenders may limit their social exposure out of fear that they will be reincarcerated for allegedly violating the terms of their release when they have not. Perceived unfair treatment while under supervision may add to the negative feelings offenders have toward the justice system.

Negative feelings toward supervision may cast a shadow over the treatment setting. Clients' attitudes toward treatment range from acceptance and the hope that it might help, to resentment when treatment is viewed as just another means of punishment. Clients often feel they don't need treatment and view it as another hoop they must jump through to complete probation. Some clients are able to attend treatment while in custody but may still be required to attend treatment post-release.

In the treatment setting, the clinician typically maintains contact with the client's supervisor to update them on the offender's progress. Supervisors often have expectations related to treatment and treatment providers. Community custody supervisors may view treatment through the community supervision lens. This can result in a belief that treatment should be conducted in a manner that is more punitive and confrontational. Expectations may extend to the length of time clients spend in treatment; they may question treatment programs where clients have completed treatment too quickly.

Offenders are typically required to undergo periodic polygraph examinations. These have been shown to be effective in helping to curtail behavior that is in violation of their conditions of release. Disclosure of violations are not uncommon. If offenders are found to have violated the conditions of their release, punishment for the violation may follow and the clinician advised. The threat of being violated is usually the greatest concern of clients who are under supervision. Fear of being violated may create a kind of double-bind. Clients are encouraged to disclose troubling thoughts, feelings, and behaviors, but disclosure may reveal a violation of the conditions of their release which could lead to punishment.

The clinician most often finds that the client's community supervisor is supportive of treatment goals. Their role as enforcer increases client attendance. Some clients claim that they are being treated unfairly by their supervisors. Supervisors may earn a reputation for being heavy-handed or unfair. Agencies tasked with offender supervision may develop reputations that may shade the client's view of their supervisor. Clients may enlist the help of treatment providers to intervene. In these cases, the clinician must evaluate the potential outcomes of intervention on the client.

Some clients have a history of supervisory problems. If clients are thought to be partly causing these problems, this is more "grist for the mill." If the clinician and community supervisor have a good alliance, discussion can lead to insights into the dynamics of all parties and ways to best address client issues.

Therapeutic Alliance

Each clinician comes to treatment with a unique background and personality. Many providers have witnessed or experienced sexual abuse. Many have strong feelings about sexual abuse and those who perpetrate it. It is part of the human condition to have such feelings. In the terminology of the workbook, our emotional brains are wired to react to sexual experiences. Often these experiences continue to exert their influence subconsciously.

It is easy to see in some treatment material a disdain for the client. The repeated references to their "deviance" and "multiple offenses" betray the bias of the author. In some treatment programs, clients engage in exercises that seem to be designed to humiliate rather than educate. Clients complain that the treatment setting is abusive, and their resistance to treatment increases.

One suspects that such treatment arises from a need to punish the offender. When treatment becomes about punishment, the therapeutic alliance ceases to exist. Negative feelings toward clients may lead to other treatment abuses. How many clients have been labeled "unamenable to treatment" due to the negative treatment setting? How many treatment programs lack clear objectives and reasonable disclosure of length of treatment because clients are viewed negatively?

Clinicians who struggle with a history of abuse, or have strong negative feelings about abusers, would do well to seek counseling to address those feelings. Personal history can be a valuable asset in treatment. Clinicians who have been victimized, have unique insight into the experience of victims of abuse. But this victim empathy can distort perceptions of abusers and negatively impact the clinician's treatment.

The Human Condition

Regaining Control addresses the causes of conflict we all experience. The influence of emotional impulses, needs, and cravings, on thinking and behavior, is at the heart of who we are. The emotional life is both a source of enrichment and conflict. Our thoughts may also betray a side of us we would rather deny. We, too, are prone to the fallacies that our clients use in defense of their conduct. We may not have committed the acts they have done, but we all know the feeling of shame and guilt that accompany behavior that we wish had never happened. Our clients often show our own struggles drawn large.

As therapists we use this common human experience as the basis for providing compassionate support. We sit in the therapist's chair not because we have never struggled, but by virtue of our insight into our own failures. We can support clients even as we work to gain greater mastery over our emotional brains. Our empathy for their struggles is the basis for "unconditional positive regard."

Most clients come to treatment wondering how they ever got to this point. They question the dichotomy between how they perceive themselves and their actions. They wonder what they were thinking—or why they weren't thinking—at the time of their offense. This duality between thinking and feeling that leads to harmful action is at the core of the human condition. As humans, we simply are not reasoning computers who always strive to maximize the good. We are also selfish, petty, vengeful, and reckless.

Recognizing that this cognitive-emotional conflict is a fact in all our lives, *Regaining Control* gives clients tools to yield greater control to their executive processes. It does so first by helping clients recognize the signs of the emotional brain at work. Secondly, clients consider the executive brain's functions and how they can regulate emotional states. Finally, *Regaining Control* examines how emotions can be used in concert with thinking to produce positive action.

Treatment Goals

"No more offenses" remains the primary goal of treatment. How best to achieve this goal is a matter of ongoing investigation. The Good Lives model suggests that the more positives a client has in their life, the less likely they are to engage in actions that put them at risk. Many clients state that their offense occurred during a period when their life was not going well. In terms of the emotional brain, the more positive emotions (optimism, hope, contentment, satisfaction) a client experiences, the less likely they are to pursue activities associated with negative feelings of the past. When clients learn to manage feelings to pursue positive goals, they experience a sense of control that encourages further mastery.

It is critically important that clients construct their own goals. The exercise of forming goals is an important function of executive thinking and one that can be developed with practice. Some clients are reluctant to set goals due to the fear of failure. Others believe the effort is pointless as their status as a sex offender prohibits them from pursuing the goals they value. Most clients can agree to setting basic goals such as completing treatment, attending sessions, and completing workbook assignments. As clients achieve basic goals, they can begin to look further into the future. The client's struggle with goals is used to illustrate the shift of control from the emotional brain to the executive. They practice commitment when their emotional brain wants to give up. With the achievement of goals comes a sense of accomplishment. When clients experience obstacles when trying to accomplish goals, they learn to recognize the emotional experience and use the tools learned in treatment to persevere. Clients learn to revise goals and strategies to achieve them.

Self-efficacy and Locus of Control

Self-efficacy refers to an individual's sense of control or mastery of life's circumstances. Individuals high in self-efficacy might be called optimists. Self-efficacy, is usually the product of achievement. As we accomplish tasks, we are encouraged to take on other challenges. As we overcome obstacles, we feel a greater confidence in our ability to meet future challenges. Sometimes this process includes failures, and more critically, our ability to recover and accomplish goals in spite of failed attempts. Treatment is designed to bolster a client's sense of self-efficacy with respect to problem behaviors. If treatment is effective, clients complete it feeling more confident that they will not reoffend.

Regaining Control approaches self-efficacy on many fronts. It helps clients uncover and evaluate thoughts, feelings, and behaviors that have been self-defeating. It encourages clients to evaluate past experience—successes and failures—to learn from these and to formulate positive goals and develop effective strategies to accomplish them. As clients work through challenges, the hope is that they will grow more confident in their ability to make meaningful changes in their lives.

Most adult offenders lived independently prior to their offense. Many had steady employment, stable families, and active community lives. During incarceration, offenders are stripped of most decision making. They are tasked with adhering to rigid rules. Upon release, they continue to live under a set of rules that govern much of their existence. The justice system acts as a parent, rewarding and punishing clients for their obedience or disobedience to rules. Treatment can be viewed as a process by which clients internalize those rules that are beneficial to them. As clients evaluate their own ethical standards and take responsibility for their conduct, the locus of control shifts from the supervisor to them.

Stories

Every client has a story to tell. They come to treatment with a unique history and interpretation of it. In the post-modern era, where facts seem to elude us and our presentation of self through social media has taken on a new meaning, personal storytelling has new significance. Some clients' stories serve to lessen guilt by shifting the responsibility of their actions onto others—victims, family members, society, or drugs. Other stories seem to have the opposite purpose—intensifying guilt and shame by exaggerating the negative effects of their offense. Most clients' stories diverge to some degree from the official records captured in police reports. Clinicians are tasked with seeing through the stories clients tell.

In *Regaining Control,* client stories are viewed as an attempt to form a narrative that is consistent with the client's self-image. Clients who shift blame, rationalize, or employ other defense mechanisms, may be communicating that the conduct of which they were accused is abhorrent to them. Their story usually implies that they care about the way they are perceived by others and are seeking approval. Many other messages may be inferred from a client's narrative and should be explored in treatment.

But what of clients who deny their offense? Clients may say that they pleaded guilty to reduced criminal charges upon advice of their attorney to avoid a more harsh sentence. In some cases, this is in fact the truth. But what of those who refuse to admit the truth? Those whose story is patently false? Should this story be confronted until the client admits the truth?

Regaining Control suggests that we all create narratives or stories in an effort to explain our experience. These explanations are the product of both the emotional and executive brains. Emotions color and filter our perceptions of events. They also influence the way memories are reconstructed in our recalling of them. During treatment, clients discuss the basis of their stories. They consider alternate narratives that might be more helpful in reaching their goals. Dispassionate evaluation of experience and associated memories may help them to form a more accurate picture. In an accepting environment, clients learn that the truth, though painful at times, is the best starting point for constructing a better future.

In treatment, clients work to become more empathetic. They are asked to take differing perspectives— witnesses, victims, law enforcement, probation/parole, family members, and fictional characters. By taking these perspectives, clients learn to question their own perceptions and memories. Clients who begin treatment convinced that they have done nothing wrong, often begin to see how their actions could appear otherwise. Most clients can at least accept that their actions contributed to an environment where they could be accused.

Treatment can be viewed as an opportunity for clients to reshape their narratives. *Regaining Control* helps them rewrite their stories. Clients often begin treatment with victim narratives: the system is unfair, their victim lied, their attorney was incompetent, family members set them up, and so on. They may view themselves as downtrodden, abused, and suppressed. Some may have some justification for this view. During treatment, they are asked to change their view of themselves from victim to survivor. As clients succeed, they begin to view themselves as capable individuals who can change and have a good life. They can become a success story, as they define it.

The Limits of Change and Sexual Schema

Regaining Control states that most clients can make significant positive changes in their lives. But change is contingent on the client's effort and ability. The brain's plasticity is viewed as the basis for change. As clients learn the material in the workbook and apply it to their lives, their brain changes. Change is nothing more than altering neural connections to facilitate modified thoughts, feelings, and behaviors. The result is the client feels a greater sense of control over thoughts and feelings that once contributed to their offense. But clinicians must also accept the fact that there are limits to the degree to which the brain can modify its neural connections. Some clients conclude treatment wondering why they ever acted as they did. Others, must accept that they will always struggle with impulses to act out. For these clients, learning to manage thoughts and feelings is the best they can hope for.

Regaining Control calls the client's sexual preferences and interests their *sexual schema*. Sexual schemas are thought to include a type of composite of many aspects of anatomy available to the senses—body shape, skin quality, color, size, sexual maturity, and so on. It is thought that clients evaluate others through the filter of this schema, comparing preferred anatomy to determine degree of fit. Checking for fitness includes evaluating behaviors that indicate sexual responsiveness. This process is thought to occur habitually, subconsciously, and universally. Though sexual schema mature with the individual, it likely retains a core set of criteria.

Though the sexual schema remains relatively fixed as we mature, events can influence its formation—especially during "critical periods." During adolescence, as youth experience the changes brought on by increasing hormones, sexual preferences may be more fluid. Experimentation is common as individuals explore a range of sexual experience in pursuit of their preferences. Some evidence suggests that exposure to stimuli during this period has a greater degree of influence on the person's persisting sexual interests. Some clients may form paraphilias as they make this transition to adulthood.

Though further research is needed, it appears that sexual schema are largely a matter of genetics and are set, in some cases, before a child is born. It further appears that these areas of the brain are more resistant to modification. This can be seen in clients who have differing gender identification, preference, or orientation. Pedophiles are also likely to have associated neurological differences.

Most clients show preferences for a specific range of sexual experience. Heterosexual men, for example, typically prefer pornography depicting females (males with females or females with females). The heterosexual male is unlikely to explore gay sexual images. In treatment, most clients say they found bondage or role playing with partners to be unsatisfying. Though clients may stray outside their preferred experience (clients often say this was the case with their offense), this may be viewed as an aberration from an otherwise "normal" sexual schema. Child pornography users may say they viewed the illegal pornography by accident, and then only briefly out of curiosity.

While *Regaining Control* asserts that clients can learn to control impulses to act out, it must be recognized that this may not be the case for all clients. Some clients simply choose not to manage these behaviors. Others may struggle to manage them and consistently fail. Though there is more study to be done, it seems clear that some clients suffer from neurological deficits that make executive control over harmful behaviors virtually impossible. Thankfully, a very small percentage of clients fall into this category.

Overview of Chapters

Workbook chapters can be grouped into clusters. Each cluster's primary focus is listed in the heading in bold. Chapters usually contain a degree of overlap with other clusters as well. The groupings below are suggestions for the clinician to consider when assigning chapters. Chapters in Part 2 can be assigned in any order the clinician or client choose. Some chapters are clearly sequential and it is recommended to assign them in order as presented in the workbook. The Regaining Control Database, available through the publisher's website, has tools to facilitate the setting up and tracking of client programs, including assigning chapters by cluster. Clusters are listed below with their chapters.

Prior Treatment Cluster (Chapters 1, 2)

The chapters in this cluster address the purpose and benefits of treatment and expectations of group members. It assumes the client has either not participated in treatment before or has reservations about the process.

1 Treatment that Works

This chapter introduces the interplay between thoughts, feelings, and behaviors. The goal of treatment is to raise awareness of emotional states and thinking patterns that lead to harmful behaviors. The impact of negative patterns on relationships and sex is also discussed. The chapter concludes with challenging clients to consider areas of "focus" they would like to work on.

2 Being in a Group

This chapter lists the benefits of the group experience. It explains how group works generally and the role group members play in the functioning of a group. Rules related to confidentiality, participation, honesty and accountability are also discussed.

Treatment View Cluster (Chapters 5, 8, 18)

Since most offenders are mandated to attend treatment, Regaining Control assumes group members come to treatment with a degree of negative feelings. These chapters are intended to address some of the concerns that clients may have about the treatment process.

5 Stance Toward Treatment

In Chapter 5, clients consider their perceptions of their offense including the factors that contributed to it. Many clients come to treatment stating they have been falsely accused, or the facts have been distorted. Some have pleaded guilty to an offense, fearing more severe penalties if they went to trial and lost. This chapter helps clients to share their feelings and beliefs about their circumstances. It also challenges them to begin to consider how they could address negative emotions that might hinder treatment.

8 Stages of Change

Chapter 8 introduces the transtheoretical model of change. It challenges clients to consider where they are in the change process. The process of change is used to explain how positive and negative habits form.

18 Pessimists and Optimists

Chapter 18 contrasts the optimistic view with the pessimistic view. Clients are challenged to examine their view of themselves and their circumstances to determine which of these stances fit them. Clients come to treatment with a broad range of attitudes about life after adjudication. Some believe they will never be able to live a good life again. The weight of the sex offender label is so heavy they see little reason to get on with their lives. Others are more optimistic. They believe life can resume and they can still accomplish goals. Pessimists are encouraged to see their situation more optimistically.

Goals Cluster (Chapters 6, 7, 19, 20)

Regaining Control is designed to exercise clients' executive function. Offenders often have a history of failed attempts to set and accomplish goals. These four chapters focus on developing the skills to accomplish them. Sex offender clients may find it more difficult to achieve goals due to the restrictions placed on them. Most have hopes for a better future but struggle to take positive steps to realize it. The emphasis in these chapters is not on the specific kinds of goals the client has, but on their ability to formulate goals and reasonable strategies to accomplish them. During treatment, clients are assessed as to whether they are using effective strategies to accomplish goals.

6 Forming Goals

Chapter 6 begins the discussion of goals. It discusses the benefits of setting goals and how to formulate goals that are effective. It also introduces the topic of strategies and concludes with clients filling out a goals chart. This chart can be referenced throughout treatment to assess clients' progress.

7 Resources

This chapter considers the internal and external resources available to clients to accomplish goals. Clients may come to treatment with very negative feelings about themselves and their failures. These clients are asked to look at their positive attributes. This chapter challenges clients to also consider the resources—people and institutions—that can help them accomplish goals.

19 Action Planning

This chapter looks at the process by which an impulse becomes action. As clients pursue goals, they must learn to evaluate the consequences of actions and formulate strategies to produce more positive ones. Many clients struggle to manage impulses (this is perhaps the most common characteristic of offenders in treatment). This chapter challenges clients to examine the way negative habits form and how to break them.

20 Planning Success

In this chapter, clients take another look at their goals. They consider the SWOT model and learn to consider contingencies and consequences. The chapter also address clients' attitudes toward their goals. It challenges clients to have a realistic view (realistic optimism), in contrast to an overly confident attitude with little support (super optimism). Most clients come to treatment confident they will not repeat past mistakes. This confidence is largely based on the realization that another offense will lead to incarceration. Clients are encouraged to formulate more specific strategies to avoid reoffending.

Rules (Chapter 17)

Offenders come to treatment with a history of rule breaking. They have (or are presumed to have) broken laws related to their offense. Most clients in treatment are under supervision and/or subject to conditions of release that contain rules governing many aspects of their lives. Treatment providers also have rules for participation in treatment. Clients sometimes struggle to conform to these rules. They are often seen as overly burdensome. This chapter is designed for clients who display an ongoing or extensive history of rule breaking.

17 Rules

This chapter discusses the way our executive and emotional brains handle rules. It considers how rules can be beneficial to the client. Many clients complain that the rules they must follow are onerous and unnecessary. Many clients find that they would follow many of the rules that govern their conduct now—their objection is that these rules are imposed. Clients are asked to consider those rules and to formulate their own. The intent is to shift the focus to the client's internal locus of control.

Good Life (Chapters 3, 21, 22)

Regaining Control rests on the assumption that clients can have a good life, and that pursuing a good life is more likely to lead to success in treatment and lower the risk of recidivism. Striving for a good life can help motivate clients to exercise executive functions (planning, emotional regulation). Clients who are more positively motivated are less likely to engage in behaviors that put their future at risk.

3 A Good Life

Chapter 3 challenges clients to consider their view of a good life. It asks, "What do you want out of life?" Clients are asked to consider the values and attitudes that play a part in achieving their good life. Finally, clients are tasked with resolving conflicting values.

21 Purpose

This chapter helps clients clarify their life purpose. It lists signs of life purpose and indicators of a life without purpose. It concludes with discussion of how clients can begin to find their own purpose. Purpose is viewed as the foundation on which a good life rests.

22 Back to the Good Life

The final chapter in this cluster suggests that life is most satisfying when clients refrain from repeating harmful behavior and connect with others in a positive way. The Treatment Objectives Checklist follows the chapter as the final assignment of Part 1. Here clients review (with feedback from the group/therapist) the degree to which they have accomplished the objectives listed. By the end of treatment, most clients have made some progress on accomplishing items on this list.

Background (Chapters 9, 10, 12, 13)

The chapters in this cluster focus on the client's life history and their perceptions of it. Clients often lack insight into the thoughts and feelings that contributed to harmful actions. These chapters explore the origins of some of their negative behaviors. It is hoped that by gaining a better understanding into their history, clients will be able to break cycles of behavior and negative thinking patterns that contributed to their offense.

9 Life History

This chapter examines some of the significant events that have impacted the client's life. It considers their family of origin, legal history, physical health, and concludes with considering client successes. The client usually presents this chapter early in treatment to give others in group a sense of who they are and the challenges they face. Supportive group feedback can serve to assure the client that their experience is one that is shared by others who are learning to make better choices as well.

10 My Story

Clients typically struggle with telling the stories of their offenses. This chapter urges clients to simply recount the facts in as accurate a manner as possible. Clients often digress into defenses designed to lessen the negative perceptions of their offense. The "thinking errors" that often accompany the recounting of the client's offense are addressed throughout the workbook. This presentation is focused on opening the door for resistant clients. Non-judgmental listening creates an environment where clients can share the details of their offense. Rationalizations, blaming others, and other defense mechanisms frequently come to the surface. These can be viewed as a fundamental acceptance that what occurred was wrong. As clients progress in treatment, many begin to assume a greater degree of responsibility for their actions.

12 Why I Did It

This chapter examines the thoughts and feelings that contributed to the offense. It examines how clients view themselves and their actions. The chapter concludes with a discussion of how clients can use their experience in a positive way. Many clients state their offense was atypical of who they are. They struggle to understand why they acted as they did. Confusion about their offense leads some clients to settle into a hopeless/helpless orientation. A significant number of clients struggle with this chapter as they are still in denial of their offense. It seems clear that some offenders have taken a plea to reduced charges, fearing a harsher sentence. For these clients, the focus of this chapter can be on the positive benefits they can still achieve through treatment. For deniers, the chapter can be approached as answering the question, "Why I was accused." Most deniers admit that their actions created an opportunity where they could be accused.

13 Needs and Sex

This chapter explores the interplay between needs and emotions. It contends that negative emotions can distort needs, resulting in attitudes and behaviors that cause harm in a relationship. The chapter concludes with an overview of how distorted needs can lead to harmful sexual acting out.

Mental Health (Chapter 11)

Regaining Control assumes that the brain is responsible for the choices client's make. It does not take a position on the existence of the soul or spirit and, in fact, accepts a number of beliefs that are shown to be useful in treatment even though they have limited empirical support. By focusing on the brain, the workbook tries to remain as neutral as possible. Clients seem to accept this explanation of behavior and find that their offense is accurately explained using the two-brain model. Though the two-brain model is discussed throughout the workbook, this chapter focuses on mental illness and its relation to offending behavior.

11 Brains and Mental Health

This chapter examines the client's mental health history. It provides a brief description of how the brain functions and factors that influence its functioning. Mental health conditions that are common among clients are listed and clients are asked to share their own life experience of mental health diagnosis and treatment. Many clients have some history of drug abuse. Many others have a history of brain trauma from sports, military service, or accidents. This chapter encourages clients to take responsibility for their mental health by seeking professional services and use of medications as prescribed.

Denial/Innocence (Chapter 4)

Though only one chapter in the workbook specifically addresses the topic of denial, the client's attitude toward their offense and other negative actions is a theme that frequently occurs in the workbook. Some clients are steadfast in their denial of their offense. Some have pleaded guilty to their offense upon advice of an attorney or to avoid trial. Some clients who initially deny their offense later admit to it. For others, denial only strengthens. The therapist sometimes must walk a difficult line—challenging clients to be honest about their actions (stop denying) while accepting that some clients have not committed the acts of which they were accused. *Regaining Control* holds that clients can still benefit from applying the principles of the workbook even if they remain in denial.

4 What if I'm Innocent?

This chapter addresses denial and the impact it has on treatment and the client's future. It lists examples of forms of denial that are often encountered in treatment. Clients are asked to consider the facts of their case from an objective juror's viewpoint. The chapter concludes with an overview of the Transtheoretical Model. The model challenges clients to view their actions and attitudes as a "work in progress." Denial is viewed as roughly equivalent to pre-contemplation.

Repetition (Chapters 25, 26, 27, 44, 45)

Regaining Control recognizes that some clients' offenses are part of a pattern or cycle of behavior, while others were a one-time event. It is broadly assumed that offenders suffer from compulsions to act out and are likely to repeat past harmful acts unless this compulsive cycle is corrected. Many treatment programs focus on addressing stimuli or triggers that are likely to induce the client to engage in harmful behavior. Similar to the drug abuse treatment model, sex crimes are seen as the consequence of persisting internal urges that must be managed. While it is often the case that client's act out under the influence of compulsion (most typically sexual), offenses are not always part of an on-going cycle. Nevertheless, the majority of clients have struggled with negative habits such as smoking, drug use, pornography use, or harmful relationship patterns. These chapters are designed for clients who have shown a pattern of repeated offenses or who struggle with compulsions/addictions. Since many clients meet this criteria, these chapters are part of most clients' treatment program.

25 Breaking Habits

This chapter discusses the process by which habits are formed. It discusses the purpose and benefits of habit formation and how clients can begin to break habits by considering consequences. Clients are asked to consider how the habit formation cycle can be utilized to break habits.

26 Chains and Cycles

In this chapter, clients practice breaking down habits in to their constituent parts. They practice identifying the thoughts and feelings that lead to behavior. Clients examine vicious and virtuous cycles and consider how to use the habit cycle in a positive way. The chapter concludes with a discussion of breaking links (thoughts and feelings).

27 Breaking Links

This chapter expands on the topic of identifying and breaking links in negative habit chains. It considers ways in which the link identification process can go wrong. The chapter discusses the use of behavioral interventions and their limitations. Thoughts and feelings are once again examined as critical pieces of behavioral change.

44 Repeat Offenders

This chapter is designed to address cycles that involve sexual offenses. It uses the Transtheoretical Model to consider how an offense cycle is born. The chapter discusses some processes that occur in the Preparation Phase such as selecting and grooming victims and keeping the offense from being discovered. Discussion of the Action Phase includes how clients' behaviors produce the offense itself. In the Maintenance Phase, the offense is justified, accommodated, and repeated.

45 Escaping the Cycle

After examining the abuse cycle, clients learn to detect indicators that they are on the path to committing another offense. Thoughts and feelings that form the beginning of a client's offense cycle are examined. Clients are then challenged to formulate a plan to address these thoughts and feelings before they result in harmful behavior. Clients often need assistance in formulating specific strategies.

Schema (Chapters 32, 33, 41, 43, 52, 53, 54, 55)

The chapters in this cluster examine the client's sexuality. Clients are asked to examine their sexual history including major events that may have helped shape their sexual interests. Clients will likely identify as heterosexual and express a primary interest in adult females. This may be due to societal and group norms, but is likely to simply represent the percentages of heterosexual adult males in the population. Men who have offended against juveniles, often state a preference for physically mature females. They may describe their victim as being fully sexually developed. True pedophiles may also engage in typical adult sexual relationships as well. Percentages of clients who struggle with sexual identity is low. Some clients say they have experimented with homosexual acts but found them unsatisfying. Clients whose offense is classified as a child offense (offense with someone under the age of consent) or who indicate an interest in sexual activity that is paraphilic, are assigned these chapters.

32 Sexual Scheming

This chapter introduces the topic of sexual schema. *Regaining Control* uses this term to refer to the client's sexual interests, identity, and preferences. It asks the client to consider the sensory data they associate with sexuality. The chapter lists some of the experiences clients may have had that helped shape their schema. Clients are also asked to consider the stimuli that activate their sexual schema. It concludes with examples of beliefs about sexuality that can lead to harmful behaviors.

33 Changing Schemas

Having identified some of the client's schema, this chapter looks further at social experiences and their impact on schema. The chapter explains that the brain "embodies" the sexual schema. The brain's schema is, in some areas, fixed before birth and is resistant to change. The chapter concludes that though a schema may be resistant to change, the client can still learn to manage the impulses that may contribute to negative behavior.

41 Bad Associations

This chapter examines the way the brain is constantly forming associations between things. Specifically, it looks at sexual associations and asks client's to consider the feelings that these associations evoke. It concludes with discussion of how to correct associations that are potentially harmful.

43 Sex and Offenses

This chapter considers what motivates people to commit sex offenses. Motivators range from biological processes to social messages. Clients are asked to increase awareness of these messages and to assume greater executive control of their responses.

52 Developing Brains

This chapter discusses factors that can influence how the brain develops sexual interests. The developmental approach considers critical periods in maturation and the unique impacts experience can have during these periods. Maturity is viewed as the brain's ability to exercise greater executive control through neural development. It concludes with a four-step process for regaining control.

53 Paraphilias

This chapter reviews various types of paraphilias most often found in treatment and how they can begin. It looks at the typical "arousal template" and its evolutionary purpose. Clients consider whether they have sexual interests that qualify as paraphilic. The chapter concludes with a discussion of ways to manage paraphilias.

54 Nature Versus Nurture

In this chapter, clients consider their genetic heritage and impacts of socialization on their sexual interests. Their own victimization (if it occurred) and the impact of abuse on others is discussed. The chapter concludes with a discussion of the nature of brain change and managing paraphilias.

55 Disease and Choice

This chapter considers the client's ability to change sex offending behavior. It considers the question of whether sex offenses are the product of disease or choice. The chapter states that some people are more predisposed to commit a sexual offense, but that they still have a choice. Clients who are more predisposed are advised to make a plan to address problem thoughts and feelings.

Relationships and Sex (Chapters 14, 15, 16)

Many clients say that at the time of their offense, they were having difficulties in a significant relationship. Others say they have experienced a series of troubled relationships or never had a long-lasting one that was satisfying. This cluster of chapters examines the role of sex in relationships.

14 Sex and Healthy Relationships

This chapter looks at the role of sex in a healthy relationship. Clients are asked to consider the emotional and physical aspects of sex. The chapter continues with considering signs that a relationship is suffering and concludes with asking clients to consider what they really want in a relationship.

15 Sexual Beliefs

This chapter asks the client again to consider their beliefs and attitudes about sex. It contrasts emotional beliefs that can be harmful with healthy ones. Clients are asked to evaluate their beliefs and determine whether their beliefs are consistent with their conduct.

16 Sex in Relationships

In this chapter, the physiology of love is discussed as a way to emphasize the body's influence over executive function. It traces the phases of physiology from lust to attachment and rejection. The chapter concludes with discussion of the problems that can arise when people base a relationship on sex, and offers alternative expressions of sexuality.

Pornography (Chapters 48, 49, 50)

It is a safe assumption that all clients have had some exposure to pornography. Most clients admit to occasional use of porn, some with the support and participation of partners. Most clients indicate that pornography has not had a significant negative impact on their relationships. Clients are typically under continuing supervision while in community treatment and are prohibited from the use of pornography. Most treatment providers also prohibit its use under the theory that pornography may tempt the client to engage in problem behaviors. While the effects of pornography use can be debated, the client's adherence to the prohibition against pornography can serve as a marker of executive control. The plethora of soft and hard porn images in our culture provide a rich environment for clients to notice their reactions to these images and develop strategies to regulate their responses.

48 Pornography

This chapter examines what is meant by the term pornography. The focus of the chapter is on images rather than on other media (written, music, etc.) since this is the media most often accessed by men. It discusses the potential issues partners raise when pornography use is occurring. The chapter looks at the Transtheoretical Model to explain how pornography use can turn to addiction. It concludes with discussion of the signs of porn addiction.

49 Porn Progression

This chapter continues the discussion of pornography addiction. It introduces a seven-layer model of addiction to explain the progression from exposure to addiction. This cycle is explored and used to suggest areas where interventions could be most effective. The chapter concludes with a look at how relationships are portrayed in pornography and asks if the client's relationships reflect some of these qualities.

50 Masturbation and Imagination

This chapter explores the client's practice of masturbation. It recognizes that masturbation is a common experience for men and focuses on the thoughts and feelings associated with it. The focus is on avoiding potentially harmful thoughts and fantasies that might be reinforced by the pleasure of orgasm. It also encourages clients to avoid masturbatory behaviors that are risky (masturbation in public restrooms, online exposure, etc.) and behaviors that were associated with their offense.

Cognitive Distortions (Chapters 23, 24, 28, 42, 51)

Regaining Control rests on several assumptions related to cognition. First it assumes that most clients' offenses are viewed negatively by the clients themselves—at least by the time they have completed treatment. Therefore, it is safe to assume that clients have engaged in efforts to rationalize their behavior prior to their offense, following their offense, or both. It is also assumed that the motivations for their behavior are "emotional" and that emotional experience is largely responsible for this cognitive accommodation for their actions. This rationalizing of behavior is often evident in other areas of the client's experience and may come to light during incarceration or supervision. This cluster focuses on how the emotional brain interacts with the executive brain to distort thinking.

23 Emotional Thinking

This chapter examines the interplay between the emotional and executive brains. It examines how emotions color thoughts and shape our perceptions. It concludes with a five-step process for making decisions and dealing with consequences of choices. Clients are taught that "overriding" emotions can often lead to better outcomes.

24 Emergency Cures for Emotional Thinking

This chapter focuses on practical steps a client can take to deal with strong emotions. It begins with a discussion of signs that indicate a client is under the influence of emotions. The chapter continues with strategies clients can use to address negative emotions in the moment. It concludes with more strategies that might assist the client avoid emotional emergencies in the future.

28 Where Thoughts Lie

This chapter asks clients to examine the role of thoughts and how they govern behavior. It asks clients to consider their feelings about some of the ideas they value. The chapter concludes that we all have a tendency to lie to ourselves when doing so is seen to have a benefit. Clients are asked to play detective and ferret out the truth of a hypothetical example and examples from their own lives.

42 Sexual Thought Viruses

This chapter examines client beliefs and feelings about sex. It suggests that attitudes and beliefs about sex are like viruses—caught and spread with little awareness. In line with the metaphor, clients are advised that they must actively resist invasion by being aware of the messages they are receiving and challenging them.

51 Arousing Curves

In this chapter, clients look at the influence of emotions on thinking. The chapter uses the Arousal Curve to show that as emotions increase in intensity, rational thought decreases. Many clients state that at the time of their offense, they weren't thinking. This chapter offers an explanation for this experience and suggests steps to counter this loss of control in the future through the exercise of executive function. It suggests the most effective time for executive intervention—as early in the curve as possible.

Shame (Chapters 29, 30, 31)

Most clients experience a significant degree of guilt and shame. The justice system and society reinforces these negative feelings. Even among the incarcerated, sex offenders are viewed as the lowest of the low. *Regaining Control* considers the utility of shame as a motivator to change. Unfortunately, some clients' experience of shame is so severe they lack the motivation to change. Some believe that their actions disqualify them from ever having a good life again. This cluster of chapters addresses those who are so plagued with guilt they find no reason to do the work of treatment.

29 Barriers to Change

This chapter considers the reasons people refuse, or seem unable, to change. It begins with discussion of attitudes about change and the reasons clients give to resist it. Clients are asked to consider the possible consequences of making changes in their lives. It concludes with discussion of how to make change positive by pursuing positive goals.

30 Shame

This chapter considers the purpose of shame as a motivator to doing better. It compares shame and the inner voice that is like a harshly critical coach. Clients are asked to consider the messages they tell themselves. The chapter concludes with a look at using shame as a motivator to set in motion a virtuous cycle of change.

31 Forgiveness

This chapter begins by looking at the brain's ability to inflict pain on itself and others. Shame is seen as a neurological state of self-inflicted pain. Clients are asked to consider forgiveness for themselves and others as a way to move beyond the paralysis of shame into achieving change. Clients write out a statement of forgiveness from their victim's perspective as a way to begin moving forward.

Fantasy (Chapters 34, 35)

Fantasy plays a role in many offenses. Some clients indicate that their offense was an enactment of sexual encounters they had imagined or viewed. Others say they fantasized about sexual activity that was illegal, though they never acted on these thoughts. It could be argued that most offenses were the fruit of at least a brief period of fantasy. The majority of clients are likely to deny engaging in an overly active fantasy life. *Regaining Control* states that sexual fantasy can be viewed as a kind of practice or rehearsal and therefore must be kept within healthy bounds

34 Imagination

This chapter considers the link between the brain's reward system and learning. Clients consider how pairing positive reward with imagination can lead to addiction. The chapter concludes with asking the client to use their imagination to set positive goals.

35 The Pursuit of Pleasure

This chapter looks further at the drives and rewards the brain experiences and their contribution to the novelty seeking cycle. The role of sex in the novelty seeking cycle is discussed with its ability to lead to unhealthy and illegal behavior. The "law of diminishing returns" or habituation is viewed as the basis for clients seeking novelty. Since rewards diminish for repeated behaviors, some clients seek out exaggerated behaviors in pursuit of a more stimulating reward.

Incest (Chapters 36, 37)

These two chapters are assigned to client's who have a family history of incest. Some offenders who commit incest have been the victim of incestuous sexual abuse themselves. Others offended against family members though they were not themselves victims. Many clients have witnessed incest but did not offend against family members. Among clients who have experienced incest, many relate a pattern within their family that spans generations. This cluster looks at how incest can become perpetuated in families and how clients who have been victims of incest can address their experience.

36 Family Cycles and Incest

This chapter examines the cycle of incest. It discusses the family dynamics that allow it to continue. Clients are asked to consider various mental strategies victims use to cope with incest. The effects of incest are considered for both the perpetrator and victim. The chapter concludes with methods that can be used to stop the cycle of incest.

37 The Abuse Survivor's Perspective

This chapter looks at the emotional and behavioral problems survivors of sexual abuse experience. It discusses factors that can influence how a child victim copes with abuse. Clients are then asked to consider the victim and survivor perspectives and identify which best fits their own experience. The chapter concludes with strategies clients can use to switch perspectives.

Rape (Chapters 38, 39, 40)

Chapters in this cluster are intended to address forced sex rather than consensual sex with underage victims. Most clients will likely deny that force was used to commit their offense. Many clients say their victim sent mixed signals or even initiated sex, but later fabricated a rape scenario to address questions from others (parents, boyfriends, etc.). It is unlikely that any client will openly advocate for the acceptability of rape.

38 Feelings and Rape

This chapter considers how victims of rape may feel following an assault. It examines how the feelings and thoughts an offender has about sexual violence can lead to harmful behavior, including rape. The chapter concludes by considering how clients can use the thought-feeling-behavior connection to avoid harming others in the future.

39 Beliefs and Rape

In this chapter, clients examine their beliefs related to rape. These include beliefs about the victims of rape and beliefs about themselves as rapists. Since many clients don't consider their beliefs related to rape, they are asked to look at their beliefs and consider the consequences they bring into their lives. The chapter concludes by discussing how clients can challenge harmful beliefs.

40 Setups, Traps, and Controls

This chapter begins with consideration of the brain's neurological connections used in sex and violence. It considers how sex abusers prepare, carry out, and attempt to conceal their crimes. It concludes with a look at signs that might indicate a client is at higher risk of committing another offense.

Sex Addiction (Chapters 46, 47)

The chapters in this cluster focus on the client's compulsive need to engage in activities that satisfy sexual feelings. It is often assumed that offenders commit offenses out of an overwhelming sexual impulse. Most clients deny that their offense was the result of having such an overwhelming drive for sex. Some do identify as sex addicts. *Regaining Control* believes that healthy sex can still be a part of the client's life. Healthy sex is defined as being consensual, law-abiding, occurring in a committed relationship, respecting boundaries, and respecting the physical safety of others.

46 Sex Addiction – Beginnings

This chapter asks clients to look at indicators that suggest they are in the grip of sexual addiction. It describes the signs of addiction that have been used to address drug addiction and compares these to sexual addiction. The chapter goes on to explore how sex addiction can develop and concludes with suggestions for dealing with sexual addiction.

47 Sexual Addiction and Personal Beliefs

This chapter examines the beliefs client's hold that may contribute to sexual addiction. It looks at the client's self-image and the impact of poor self-image on relationships. It considers how the role of sex can become distorted in relationships. Clients are tasked with exploring alternatives to sex to satisfy relational needs.

Emotions (Chapters 56, 57, 58, 59, 60)

Throughout the workbook the interplay between emotions and thinking are discussed. This cluster considers the emotions that arise instinctively and contrasts those with emotions we learn to associate with experiences. Many clients view emotions as largely under the direction of outside forces. During treatment, they learn to recognize the role their thoughts and behaviors play in heightening or diminishing them. Clients learn that through practice, they can exercise greater control over emotions. Clients explore how life experience has shaped their emotional experience. Many clients say their offense occurred when their emotions overrode their thinking.

56 Reflex Emotions and EQ

This chapter introduces the notion of emotional intelligence and reflex emotions—emotions that seem to be universally shared and arise without having to be learned. It continues with a discussion of two strategies to address emotions—avoidance and approach. *Regaining Control* recognizes that clients generally want to avoid repeating past harmful behaviors. But the desire to avoid repeating mistakes is not always enough. Finding positive replacements to replace unwanted behaviors is helpful. The chapter concludes with consideration of sex as an emotion and its influence on decision making.

57 Learned Emotions and EQ

This chapter discusses the process by which emotions are linked with experience. Clients consider examples in their lives that illustrate the emotional learning process. The chapter concludes by detailing how thoughts, feelings, and behaviors interact to shape our experience. The message of the chapter is that troubling emotional reactions can often be changed through intentional effort.

58 Managing Learned Emotions – Part 1

This chapter looks at a four-step process that describes how emotions are associated with experience. These steps include: having an experience, evaluation of the experience, association of feelings based on evaluation, and storage of experience and feelings in memory. By breaking apart these usually unconscious processes, client's begin to feel confident in their ability to manage emotions.

59 Managing Learned Emotions – Part 2

This chapter examines in more detail the final step in the emotional learning process—memory. The way memories are formed and how they are distorted is discussed. Clients consider how their memories of their offense may have changed. The chapter considers how clients can learn from future experiences. It concludes with suggestions for being more objective about life experience and correcting mistaken memories.

60 EQ and Strong Emotions

The influence of strong emotions on decision making is discussed in this chapter. The fight, flight, and freeze emotions are addressed along with techniques clients can use to manage them. The effects of stress and the mind-body loop are also discussed.

Empathy (Chapters 61, 62, 63, 65)

It is generally assumed that those who commit sexual offenses have deficits in empathy. It is reasoned that if offenders had a greater sense of the negative impacts of their actions on others, they would not be as likely to commit future offenses. The chapters in this cluster also focus on ethics which can be viewed as the executive brain's contribution to moral conduct. The approach examines the neurological basis for empathy—mirror neurons—and their role in shaping ethical behavior.

61 Ethical Reasoning and Empathy

This chapter considers signs of ethical and unethical behavior. It challenges clients to consider the consequences of their actions before taking action. It further asks clients to explore the inner conflict that exists when they are faced with difficult ethical choices.

62 Fighting the Good (Ethical) Fight

This chapter asks the client to consider the value of making ethical choices even when there is no obvious reward for doing so. It considers the higher reasons for positive action such as demonstrating character and remaining true to their higher beliefs. The chapter concludes with an examination of strategies clients can use to prevent unethical behavior.

63 Empathy – Feeling for Others

This chapter discusses the way the brain creates the experience of empathy. It examines the effect of client history on their experience of emotions. The chapter continues with discussion of how our perceptions of others can be distorted when we assume others are, or should be, like us. The chapter concludes with discussion of ways to detect possible areas of distortion and strategies to correct them.

65 Regaining Trust

Offenders often lament the lack of trust they experience post-offense. This chapter challenges clients to exercise empathy as they consider the reasons for this lack of trust. It considers strategies clients can use to begin to rebuild trust. Clients are confronted by the fact that trust must be earned by engaging in actions that provide proof of their commitment to change.

Self-Image (Chapters 64, 66)

This cluster of chapters considers the client's view of himself. Many clients struggle to reconcile their self-image with their actions. Many say their offense was not characteristic of them and they don't know why they committed their offense. Clients' experiences post-offense, reinforce many negative messages about who they are. *Regaining Control* helps clients to confront their harmful behaviors honestly so they can avoid repeating them. This honest self-evaluation is more than feeling remorse, shame, and guilt. Clients are encouraged to set out a path to a better life, because they are more than their failures.

64 Me in the Mirror

This chapter considers the role of memory and the client's past in the formation of their self-image. It considers how their own mirror neurons may have incorrectly contributed to a negative self-image by receiving negative messages from others. The chapter challenges clients to examine memories to see themselves more objectively.

66 Changing Focus

The final chapter in the workbook asks clients to compare their self-image now with who they were at the time of their offense. Clients almost always concede that they have changed during treatment (and often while incarcerated). They typically say they are less judgmental, more understanding, less selfish, and are more accountable for their actions. Clients are asked to consider how they can use their experience for the betterment of others.

Forms

Chapter Presentation

The Chapter Presentation worksheet provides an outline clients may use for written assignments or oral presentations to a group. While many clients simply choose to answer chapter questions, some find it helpful to organize their thoughts using this form. Answers should show good understanding of chapter concepts as well as their application to the client's life.

The Chapter Presentation Worksheet is shown on the following pages. Make additional copies of this form as needed.

Chapter Presentation

Client's Name____ Date:_______________________

Chapter:____

      Read through the chapter, then use the spaces below to summarize what you have learned.

Main points of the chapter:

____

____

____

____

____

____

____

What I learned about myself and others from this chapter:

____

____

____

____

____

____

How I can apply this chapter to my life, and how it might help others:

____

____

____

This chapter applies to my goals in the following ways:

Goals Chart

The Goals Chart is discussed in chapter 6, Forming Goals. Forming and accomplishing goals is a very important part of treatment. Many clients find as they begin to accomplish goals they are more willing to establish new goals and their list of goals expands. Since goals are a work in progress, they often need to be revised. Clients will likely need to make several copies of their goals as they progress.

The Goals Chart is shown on the following page. Make additional copies of this form as needed.

Goals Chart

Goal Name:	Goal Strategies	Target Date	Done?

My SWOT Plan

My SWOT Plan is discussed in Chapter 20, Planning Success. Each goal listed in the Goals Chart will be the subject of a SWOT Plan. For example, if a client had seven goals, they would complete seven My SWOT Plan forms—one for each goal.

My SWOT Plan is shown on the following page. Make additional copies of this form as needed.

My SWOT Plan

Goal - List one of your treatment goals below. Remember to be specific. Include the 5 Ws. (See chapter 6)

Strengths - List your strengths and how you can use them to accomplish your goals. Include inside and outside resources.

Weaknesses - List personal challenges related to this goal, and say how you can use your strengths to manage them.

Opportunities - List the opportunities in your life you could take advantage of to accomplish your goals.

Threats - List the things inside and outside you that could keep you from reaching this goal. Say how you will address them.

Cycle Analysis

The Cycle Analysis form is used to outline a cycle or a chain of events. The following gives an example of a partially completed cycle analysis.

Cycle Analysis Form

Client Name:___ *Joe Smith*________ Cycle Name:__________*Argument over money with girlfriend*_________

Initiator:______*Don't have enough money to pay for bills at end of month*________________________________

Terminator:________*One of us leaves the house*____

Person(s)	Thoughts/Emotions/Behaviors
I	Get upset about not having enough money
I	Blame girlfriend for spending too much money
Girlfriend	Blames me for not working enough
We	Yell and sometimes get physical
I	Storm out of the room
Girlfriend	Calls the police and complains about me

The form is filled out as follows:

Cycle Name: This is a name that describes the cycle such as "Argument over money with girlfriend" in the example.

Initiator: This is what starts the cycle. It can be internal (ex. sexual fantasy) or external (ex. viewing pornography)

Terminator: The terminator is what concludes the cycle. In the example, "One of us leaves the house" is the terminator.

Person(s): The subject is the one doing the action. In the example, I, Girlfriend, and We are examples of the subject.

Thoughts/Emotions/Behaviors: These are the actions or feelings that occur. In the example, these are listed as: Get upset about not having enough money, Blame girlfriend for spending too much, etc.

Cycles should be written in sequence – the top row describes what happens first, the bottom row lists what happens last.

The Cycle Analysis form is designed to help clients break down a cycle into specific steps. Rather than just viewing an event as a whole (a fight), they work to break down the event into many smaller events (getting angry, yelling, walking away.). The Cycle Analysis form also helps the client separate their thoughts, feelings, and behaviors from other persons in the cycle. They begin to view themselves as an individual who responds to, or evokes responses in others.

The goal of the Cycle Analysis form is to break each action into smaller units. As the client continues to expand the Cycle Analysis, they often discover critical links of thoughts, feelings, and behaviors that feed the cycle. These links then become new points where the cycle can be broken.

The Cycle Analysis form is shown on the next page. Make additional copies of this form as needed.

Cycle Analysis

Client Name:_______________________ Cycle Name:_____________________________

Initiator:____

Terminator:____

Person	Thoughts/Emotions/Behaviors

Statement of Forgiveness

The Statement of Forgiveness form provides clients with an opportunity to express their feelings about their offense. Most offenders are prohibited from having contact with their victims and therefore never have an opportunity to get closure. Many wish they could express how sorry they are for their actions. Others have questions they would like to ask of their victim. Still others wonder how their victim is faring in life and wonder if their actions have had a negative impact on them.

This worksheet allows offenders to express their feelings and ask for forgiveness from others they have hurt without actually confronting them. **Note: this form is not to be given or shared with the victim if prohibited by the conditions of the offenders release or if victim does not consent**. If contact with the victim is allowed, the form may be shared under the supervision of therapists/guardians of the victim if the victim consents.

The Statement of Forgiveness form is not intended to be an opportunity for the client to justify their actions or place blame on the victim. The goal is for the client to assume responsibility for the actions and demonstrate empathy for the harm they may have caused. The client should also express some understanding of how they will modify their behavior in the future. Clinician's may ask that the statement be revised if the client is clearly being manipulative or lacks accountability for their offense.

Statement of Forgiveness

Describe what happened: what you would like forgiveness for.

____

____

____

Explain how you feel about what happened.

____

____

____

Write the words you would like to hear from the person you hurt, or write the words you want to tell yourself.

____

____

____

Write a statement about how you will act in the future.

____

____

____

____

Statement of Forgiveness - Example

Describe what happened: what you would like forgiveness for.

I got drunk one night and touched my niece. I told her it was okay, but I knew it wasn't. I also told her not to tell anyone else or she would get in trouble. I got arrested after she reported it.

Explain how you feel about what happened.

I feel terrible about what happened. She was too young to understand what happened. I just hope she is doing okay. She didn't deserve what happened. I know what happened will affect her for life. I'm learning why I acted as I did. I'm ashamed of myself. I know I was drunk, but still, I knew better.

Write the words you would like to hear from the person you hurt, or write the words you want to tell yourself.

From my victim—What you did made me very confused. You were my favorite uncle. I know what you did was wrong and that's why you got punished. I was really upset over what happened. Now I'm doing good. I forgive you for what you did. I'm glad you are getting help and I hope you will not make the same mistake again.

Write a statement about how you will act in the future.

I will never make the same mistake again! I know what I did was wrong. Even though I was drunk at the time, I know that's no excuse. I'm still responsible for what I did. I will never repeat this again. I quit drinking and am working to change my thoughts about kids. I will never be alone with a juvenile by myself again. Period. I am getting my life back together and will do everything in my power to make sure I don't fall back into my old habits.

References

The following list of references was consulted in the creation of *Regaining Control*. These references are illustrative of commonly available texts. Research in cognitive science and brain function continues and promises to offer significant advances in treatment. The Association for the Treatment of Sexual Abusers and their affiliated chapters is a good resource for ongoing education.

Allen, S. (1998). *Dumbth: The lost art of thinking.* New York: Promethius Books.

American Psychiatric Association. (2013). *Diagnostic and statistical manual of mental disorders* (5th ed.). Washington, DC:

Anderson, N. B., & Anderson, Elizabeth P. (2003). *Emotional longevity.* New York: Viking.

Amen, D. G. (2007). *Sex on the brain: 12 lessons to enhance your love life.* New York: Harmony Books.

Aunger, R. (2002). *The electric meme: A new theory of how we think.* New York: The Free Press

Austin, J. H. (1999). *Zen and the brain.* Cambridge, MA: The MIT Press.

Austin, J. H. (2010). *Zen brain reflections.* Cambridge, MA: The MIT Press.

Bowlby, J. (1988). *A secure base.* United States: Basic Books

Bradshaw, J. (1990). *Homecoming: Reclaiming and championing your inner child.* New York: Bantam Books.

Brodie, R. (1996). *Virus of the Mind: The new science of the meme.* New York: Hay House Inc.

Burns, D. D. (1990). *The feeling good handbook.* New York: Penguin Books.

Butler G. and Hope, T. (1995). *Managing your mind: The mental fitness guide.* New York: Oxford University Press.

Canning, M. (2008). *Lust anger love: Understanding sexual addiction and the road to healthy intimacy.* Naperville, IL: Sourcebooks, Inc.

Carnes, P. (1992). *Don't call it love: Recovery from sexual addiction.* New York: Bantam Books.

Carnes, P. (2001). *Out of the shadows: Understanding sexual addiction* (3rd ed.). Minnesota: Hazelden.

Cohen, G. D. (2005). *The mature mind: The positive power of the aging brain.* New York: Basic Books.

Cozolino, L. (2002). *The neuroscience of psychotherapy: Building and rebuilding the human brain.* New York: W. W. Norton & Company.

Damasio, A. (1994). *Descartes' error: Emotion, reason, and the human brain.* New York: Avon.

Damasio, A. (2003). *Looking for Spinoza: Joy, sorrow, and the feeling brain.* New York: Harcourt Inc.

Damasio, A. (1999). *The feeling of what happens.* San Diego: Harourt Inc.

DiClemente, C. C. (2003). *Addiction and change: How addictions develop and addicted people recover.* New York: Guilford Press.

Dimeff, L. A. and Koerner, K. (2007). *Dialectical behavior therapy in clinical practice: Applications across disorders and settings.* New York: The Guilford Press.

Ekman, P. (2009). *Telling lies: Clues to deceit in the marketplace, politics, and marriage.* New York: W. W. Norton & Company

Farrelly, F. and Brandsma, J. (1974). *Provocative therapy.* Cupertino, CA: Meta Publications Inc.

Festinger, L. (1957). *A theory of cognitive dissonance.* Stanford, CA: Stanford University Press

Finkelhor, D. (1984). *Child Sexual Abuse: New Theory & Research.* New York: The Free Press.

Frankl, V. E. (1984). *Man's search for meaning.* New York: Simon and Schuster.

Goldberg, E. (2009) *The new executive brain: Frontal lobes in a complex world.* New York: Oxford.

Goleman, D. (1995). *Emotional intelligence: Why it can matter more than IQ.* New York: Bantam Books.

Goleman, D. (2006). *Social intelligence: The revolutionary new science of human relationships.* New York: Bantam Books.

Goleman, D. (1985). *Vital lies, simple truths: The psychology of self-deception.* New York: Simon and Schuster.

Harmon-Hones, E. and Mills, J. (Eds) (2006). *Cognitive dissonance: Progress on a pivotal theory in social psychology.* Washington DC: American Psychological Association

Hayes, S. C., Follette, V. M. and Linehan, M. M. (Eds) (2004). *Mindfulness and acceptance: Expanding the cognitive-behavioral tradition.* New York: The Guilford Press.

Hoenig, C. (2000). *6 essential secrets for thinking on a new level: Making decisions and getting results.* New York: MJF.

Howard, P. J. (Ed.) (2006). *The owner's manual for the brain: Everyday applications from mind-brain research (3rd Ed.).* Austin: Bard Press.

Inaba, D. S. and Cohen, W. E. (2000). *Uppers, downers, all arounders.* Ashland OR: CNS Publications Inc.

Johnson, S. (2004). *Mind wide open: Your brain and the neuroscience of everyday life.* New York: Scribner.

Kabat-Zinn, J. (1990). *Full catastrophe living: Using the wisdom of your body and mind to face stress, pain, and illness.* New York: Delacorte Press.

Kahneman, D. (2011). *Thinking fast and slow.* New York: Farrar, Straus and Giroux.

Karen, R. (1998). *Becoming attached: First relationships and how they shape our capacity to love.* New York: Oxford University Press.

Kurzweil, R. (2012). *How to create a mind: The secret of human thought revealed.* New York: Penguin Books.

Lakoff, G. and Johnson. M. (1980). *Metaphors we live by.* Chicago, IL: The University of Chicago Press.

Lakoff, G. (1987). *Women, fire, and dangerous things: What categories reveal about the mind.* Chicago: The University of Chicago Press.

LeDoux, J. (2003). *Synaptic Self: How our brains become who we are.* New York: Penguin Books.

Loftus, D. (2002). *Watching sex: How men really respond to Pornography.* New York: Thunder's Mouth Press.

Marra, T. (2005). *Dialectical behavior therapy in private practice.* Oakland, CA: New Harbinger Publications, Inc.

Mahler, M. S., Pine, F. and Bergman, A. (1975) *The psychological birth of the human infant: Symbiosis and individuation.* United States: Basic Books.

Mahoney, M. J. (2003). *Constructive psychotherapy: A practical guide.* New York: The Guilford Press.

McNally, R. J. (2005). *Remembering trauma.* Cambridge, MA: The Belknap Press.

Medina, J. (2000) *The genetic inferno: Inside the seven deadly sins.* New York: Cambridge University Press.

Miller, W. R. and Rollnick, S. (2002). *Motivational interviewing: Preparing people for change (2nd Ed.).* New York: The Guilford Press.

Ogas, O. and Gaddam, S. (2011) *A billion wicked thoughts: What the world's largest experiment reveals about human desire.* New York: Dutton

Paul, R. and Elder, L. (2006). *Understanding the foundations of ethical reasoning.* The Foundation for Critical Thinking.

Pert, C. B. (1997). *Molecules of emotion: Why you feel the way you feel.* New York: Scribner.

Prochaska, J. O., Norcross, J. C. and DiClemente, C. C. (2006). *Changing for good.* New York: Harper Collins.

Restak, R. (2003). *The new brain: How the modern age is rewiring your mind.* United States: Saint Martin's Press

Rosenthal, N. E. (2002). *The emotional revolution: How the new science of feelings can transform your life.* New York: Kensington Publishing Corporation.

Sapolsky, R. M.. (1994). *Why zebras don't get ulcers: A guide to stress, stress-related diseases, and coping.* New York: W. H. Freeman and Company.

Scarf, M. (2008). *Intimate Partners: Patterns in love and marriage.* New York: Ballantine Books

Schacter, D. L. (1996). *Searching for memory: The brain, the mind, and the past.* New York: Basic Books.

Schacter, D. L. (2001). *The seven sins of memory: How the mind forgets and remembers.* New York: Houghton Mifflin Company.

Schiraldi, G. R. (2000). *The post-traumatic stress disorder sourcebook: A guide to healing, recover, and growth.* Los Angeles: Lowell House.

Schiraldi, G. R. and Kerr, M. H. (2002). *The anger management sourcebook.* New York: McGraw Hill.

Segal, Z. V., Williams, M. G. J. and Teasdale, J. D. (2002). *Mindfulness-based cognitive therapy for depression: A new approach to preventing relapse.* New York: The Guilford Press.

Seligman, M. E. P. (1990). *Learned optimism: How to change your mind and your life.* New York: Alfred A. Knopf, Inc.

Siegel, D. J. (1999). *The developing mind: How relationships and the brain interact to shape who we are.* New York: The Guilford Press.

Skinner, K. B. (2005). *Treating pornography addiction.* Provo, UT: Growth Climate Inc.

Springer, S. and Deutsch, G. (1999) *Left brain right brain: Perspectives from cognitive neuroscience. 5th Ed.* W.H. Freeman and Company Worth Publishers.

Struthers, W. (2009). *Wired for intimacy: How pornography hijacks the male brain.* Illinois: Intervarsity Press

Tavris, C. and Aronson, E. (2007). *Mistakes were made (but not by me): Why we justify foolish beliefs, bad decisions, and hurtful acts.* New York: Harcourt, Inc.

Watkins, P. L. and Clum, G. A. (Eds).(2008). *Handbook of self-help therapies.* New York: Routledge.

Yalom, I. D (1995). *The theory and practice of group psychotherapy, 4th Ed.* New York: Basic Books.

Yalom, I. D. (1980). *Existential psychotherapy.* New York: Basic Books.

Young, J. E., Klosko, J. S. and Weishaar, M. E. (2003). *Schema therapy: A practitioner's guide.* New York: The Guilford Press.

Zander, R. S. and Zander. B. (2000). *The art of possibility.* New York: Penguin.

Zilbergeld, B. (1999). *The new male sexuality: The truth about men, sex, and pleasure (Rev. Ed).* New York: Bantam Books.

ABOUT THE AUTHOR

James Rogers, received his Master's in Counseling from Portland State University. He was a Licensed Mental Health Counselor and Certified Sex Offender Treatment Provider Affiliate in Washington State for over seven years, where he conducted individual and group counseling for adjudicated sex offenders. Jim has experience working with forensic populations and a great interest in helping clients overcome irresponsible and unhealthy sexual behavior, so they may pursue their good lives.

Prior to pursuing a career in counseling, James retired as a Lieutenant from the Vancouver Police Department where he served for twenty-five years. During his career as a law enforcement officer, he served as a crime prevention officer, DARE officer, Patrol Corporal and Sergeant, Training Coordinator, Defensive Tactics Instructor, Firearms Instructor, Internal Affairs investigator and supervisor, and Technology supervisor.

James currently resides in Washington State and enjoys traveling with his wife.